DIGITAL TRANSFORMATION OF MALAYSIAN SMALL AND MEDIUM ENTERPRISES

DIGITAL TRANSFORMATION OF MALAYSIAN SMALL AND MEDIUM ENTERPRISES

BY

FARZANA PARVEEN TAJUDEEN
Universiti Malaya, Malaysia

SEDIGHEH MOGHAVVEMI
Universiti Malaya, Malaysia

THINARANJENEY THIRUMOORTHI
Universiti Malaya, Malaysia

SEUK WAI PHOONG
Universiti Malaya, Malaysia

AND

ELYA NABILA BINTI ABDUL BAHRI
Universiti Malaya, Malaysia

emerald PUBLISHING

United Kingdom – North America – Japan – India
Malaysia – China

Emerald Publishing Limited
Emerald Publishing, Floor 5, Northspring, 21-23 Wellington Street, Leeds LS1 4DL.

First edition 2025

British Library Cataloguing in Publication Data
A catalogue record for this book is available from the British Library

ISBN: 978-1-83662-169-0 (Print)
ISBN: 978-1-83662-168-3 (Online)
ISBN: 978-1-83662-170-6 (Epub)

Printed and bound by CPI Group (UK) Ltd, Croydon, CR0 4YY

INVESTOR IN PEOPLE

CONTENTS

List of Figure and Tables *ix*
Acknowledgements *xi*

1. Empowering Malaysian SMEs: Navigating Digital Transformation for Growth and Competitiveness 1
   1. Introduction 2
      1.1. Why Digital Transformation Is Crucial for Business 2
   2. Components of Digital Transformation 4
      2.1. Core Components of Digital Transformation for SMEs 5
   3. Understanding the Malaysian SME Landscape 5
   4. Digital Transformation – Trends and Initiatives for Malaysian SMEs 7
      4.1. Government Initiatives and Support 8
      4.2. E-commerce 10
      4.3. Data Analytics and Business Intelligence 11
   5. Key Trends Shaping the Digital Transformation Journey for Malaysian SMEs 12
   6. Chapter Summary 14
   References 14

2. The Importance of SME's Digital Transformation in Promoting the Malaysian Economy 21
   1. Introduction 22
   2. Understanding the Impact of Digital Transformation on Malaysian Economy 22
      2.1. Digital Transformation Eases the Economic Transactions 23
      2.2. Digital Transformation and Return on Investment 24
      2.3. Digital Transformation and Cost Reduction 25
      2.4. Digital Transformation and Job Creation in Formal and Informal Sectors 25
      2.5. Digital Transformation and New Work Landscapes 26
      2.6. Digital Transformation and the Economies of Scale 27
      2.7. Digital Business Models and Market Structure Transition 27

2.8. Enhancing Competitiveness and the Blue Ocean Strategy 28
3. Understanding New Economic Landscape in Digitalization 28
3.1. Inception of Digital Trade and E-commerce 29
3.2. Omni-channel Approach to Sales 30
3.3. The Role of Social Media 30
3.4. AI and Automation 31
3.5. Seller and Consumer Protection in Online Transaction 33
3.6. Dynamic Relationships Between Demand, Supply, and the Enablers 33
4. Supply Side Related to Digital Transformation 36
4.1. Digital Transformation and Production Efficiency 36
4.2. Advertisement in the Digital Economy 36
4.3. Pricing and Profitability in Digital Economy 37
4.4. Delivery System in Digital Economy 38
5. Demand Side Related to the Digital Transformation 38
5.1. Increasing Consumer's Choice of Product and Services 38
5.2. Increasing Consumer's Purchasing Power 38
5.3. Increasing Consumer Awareness of the Product and Services 39
5.4. Consumer Involvement in Increasing the Product Quality 39
5.5. Reducing Asymmetric Information 39
6. Chapter Summary 39
References 40

3. Impact of Digital Transformation on Business Functional Areas of SMEs 45
1. Introduction 46
2. Digital Transformation in Business Functional Areas 47
2.1. Digital Transformation in Operations 47
2.2. Digital Transformation in Marketing 49
2.3. Digital Transformation in Customer Service 53
2.4. Digital Transformation in Accounting and Finance 56
3. Case Study: Example of Malaysian SMEs Embracing Digital Transformation: Khairul Amin Kamarulzaman @ Khairul Aming 59
3.1. The Lessons Learned and Best Practices 61
4. Chapter Summary 62
References 63

4. Digital Transformation Issues and Challenges: Solutions for Malaysian SMEs 69
1. Introduction 70
2. Digital Transformation Challenges 71

2.1. Financial Limitations 71
2.2. Lack of Digital Skills 73
2.3. Resistance of Employees to Change 75
2.4. Digital Divide Among Firms 76
2.5. Cybersecurity Issues 77
2.6. Digital Transformation Journey: Steep Learning Curve for SMEs 79
2.7. Wide Technology Options and Issues with Third-party Digital Platforms 81
2.8. Inadequate E-commerce Adoption by SMEs 82
3. Are We Really Going Green with Digital Transformation? 84
4. Chapter Summary 86
References 86

5. Nurturing Future Workforce: Enhancing SME's Readiness for Digital Transformation in Malaysia 91
1. Introduction 92
2. Digital Transformation and Skill Requirements 94
2.1. Employability and Workforce Skills 95
3. The Malaysian Workforce and Government Plans 103
3.1. SMEs in Malaysia 106
4. Chapter Summary 106
References 108

6. Digital Future of SMEs: Towards Successful Digital Transformation 113
1. Introduction 114
2. Successful Transformative Innovation 115
2.1. Google 115
2.2. Facebook 115
2.3. Netflix 116
3. Transformative Innovation and SMEs 116
3.1. Cloud Computing 117
3.2. Business Process Automation 117
3.3. Artificial Intelligence and Machine Learning 118
3.4. Cybersecurity Technologies 118
3.5. Online Payments and E-commerce Platforms 119
3.6. Virtual Workspaces and Remote Collaboration Tools 120
4. Next-Gen Solutions for SMEs 120
4.1. Generative AI 121
4.2. Blockchain 121
4.3. Internet of Things 122
4.4. The 5G Technology 122

5. Digital Transformation and Ethics 123
5.1. Cyber Ethics 123
5.2. Transparency and Cybersecurity 124
6. Ethics in AI Development and Usage 124
7. Ethical Guidelines for SMEs Considering AI Systems 125
7.1. Cyber Ethics and Initiatives in Malaysia 126
8. Making Digital Transformation a Reality for SMEs 126
9. Case Example: From One Small Hardware Store to a Billion Dollar Home Improvement Enterprise 127
9.1. Company Background 127
9.2. Power of Data Analytics at Mr.DIY 128
9.3. E-commerce @ Mr.DIY 128
9.4. Lessons Learnt 129
10. Chapter Summary 129
References 130

About the Authors 135

LIST OF FIGURE AND TABLES

FIGURE

Fig. 1. The Digital Transformation of Business Areas Among SMEs in Malaysia. 58

TABLES

Table 1. The Features of the Type of Demand and Supply Conditions in Digital Economy. 35

Table 2. Examples of Technology, Platform, and Skills. 98

Table 3. Digital Skills and Related Technologies. 99

Table 4. Microsoft Skills and Related Technologies. 100

Table 5. Communication Skills and Related Technologies. 101

Table 6. IT and Technical Skills and Related Technologie. 103

Table 7. AI and Future Technical Trends and Related Technologies. 104

ACKNOWLEDGEMENTS

We would like to acknowledge the financial support provided by the Faculty of Business and Economics Special Book Grant: UMG019I-2023.

1

EMPOWERING MALAYSIAN SMEs: NAVIGATING DIGITAL TRANSFORMATION FOR GROWTH AND COMPETITIVENESS

ABSTRACT

In the rapidly evolving business landscape, digital transformation is a fundamental strategy for ensuring competitive advantage and operational excellence. This chapter delves into the significance of digital transformation for small and medium enterprises (SMEs), focussing on its pivotal components and the specific context of Malaysian SMEs. Digital transformation is essential for SMEs to adapt to the market demands, improve customer experiences, and drive sustainable growth. The core components of digital transformation for SMEs include e-commerce integration and data analytics. These components facilitate streamlined operations, better decision-making, and improve market reach. Understanding the Malaysian SME landscape reveals a vibrant sector with diverse needs and growth potential. Digital transformation trends in Malaysia reflect a strong move towards adopting e-commerce solutions and leveraging data analytics to gain actionable insights. The chapter also examines government initiatives aimed at supporting SMEs through digital transformation, including funding programmes, training opportunities, and infrastructural improvements. The key components influencing Malaysian SMEs' digital transformation process include the increasing importance of digital consumer engagement and the integration of digital tools into traditional business models. By aligning with these strategies and leveraging government support, Malaysian SMEs could significantly enhance the competitive edge of Malaysian SMEs, positioning them for long-term success in a digitally driven market. This chapter provides a comprehensive overview of these elements, offering valuable insights into how Malaysian SMEs can embrace and benefit from digital transformation.

Keywords: Components of digital transformation; Malaysian SME; government initiatives and support; e-commerce; data analytics; business intelligence

1. INTRODUCTION

The digital transformation landscape is evolving so rapidly that it is reshaping the operational paradigms of many organizations throughout the world. With this in mind, SMEs in Malaysia have no choice but to gain a better understanding about the essence of digital transformation so as to understand its benefits for sustainable growth and competitiveness. This chapter delves into the multifaceted realm of digital transformation among Malaysian SMEs. It offers insights and perspectives on the pertinent elements that exist within this dynamic domain. The chapter explores the essence of digital transformation and its various aspects by elucidating its underlying principles, drivers, and implications within the context of Malaysian SMEs. The fundamental components of digital transformation which encompass technological advancements, organizational culture shifts, and strategic imperatives are discussed so as to provide readers with a comprehensive understanding of its transformative potential and challenges. The chapter further expounds on the definitions and characteristics of SMEs in Malaysia, thereby contextualizing their roles and significance within the broader digital transformation discourse. By examining the unique attributes, constraints, and opportunities of the SMEs, this chapter thus underscores the importance of tailoring digital transformation strategies to suit the specific needs and contexts of Malaysian SMEs. Inevitably, this chapter offers insights into the landscape of digital transformation within Malaysian SMEs, also highlighting key trends and initiatives that can shape their digital journey.

1.1. Why Digital Transformation Is Crucial for Business

The advent of technology has made the digital transformation imperative for navigating the complexities of the modern business landscape. Digital transformation is a product of the Fourth Industrial Revolution (IR 4.0). It is a paradigm shift indicating how organizations need to operate and innovate in response to the rapid advancement of digital technologies (Wang et al., 2020). As noted by Brunetti et al. (2020), digital transformation is the fundamental reorganization of current organization works. Consequently, existing business organizations have no choice but to make improvements in their operation and business models.

The evaluation and impact of digital technologies on organizational practices and societal norms have been well documented (Hokmabadi et al., 2024; Phoong et al., 2020; Wang et al., 2020). Šaković Jovanović et al. (2020) observed that digital transformation in business, especially the introduction of electronic commerce (e-commerce), was one of the most significant achievements of the 20th century. E-commerce is a concept that refers to the buying and selling of goods and services via the internet. It is commonly facilitated by digital platforms and technology tools. One of the primary advantages of e-commerce is its capacity to enhance communications between business and their suppliers, and customers. Digital platforms such as instant messaging and online portals enable organizations to establish seamless communication channels with their suppliers for the purpose of streamlining procurement processes and managing their inventories effectively (Cao et al., 2021). Real-time communication allows businesses to respond promptly to customers, market demands, as well as optimize their supply chain operations. This process allows businesses to foster a stronger relationship with their suppliers.

Another significant aspect of digital transformation is noted in the improvement from traditional payment systems to more modern transactions that are faster, more secure, and more convenient for both parties. Diverse payment options, such as digital wallets, online banking, and mobile payments reflect the transformative impact of digitalization on the payment ecosystem (Phoong et al., 2022). Digital wallets are a prominent innovation in the realm of digital payments. They offer users a convenient and secure means of conducting transactions both online and in-store. Google Pay, PayPal, Touch 'n Go, and WeChat Pay are examples of internet-based digital wallets that enable users to store their payment information securely in a digital format, thereby eliminating the need to enter credit card details for each and every subsequent transaction. Users can also make a transaction by scanning a QR code. This reduces checkout time while facilitating transactions.

The widespread adoption of mobile payment solutions has democratized access to financial services, particularly in regions with limited banking infrastructure or access to traditional payment methods. Mobile payment apps such as Alipay, Touch 'n Go, and WeChat Pay thus leverage on smartphone technology and digital wallets to facilitate peer-to-peer transactions, bill payments, and contactless payments at merchant locations. These innovations allow convenient and secure transactions as they involve contactless service and product exchange as well as payments. The benefit was especially evident during the pandemic period. This evolution of the payment system highlights the transformative potential of the digital world in revolutionizing traditional financial processes. It is thus emphasized that the accessibility of contactless payment options, such as digital wallets, mobile payments, and online payments has made business transactions more efficient, secure, and convenient for both firms and consumers.

Digital transformation transcends technological adoption; it requires a cultural shift and an organizational mindset that is willing to embrace change and innovation. The success of digital transformation rests on strong leadership, organizational support, and the commitment to continuous learning and improvement. One of the key drivers of digital transformation is the desire to remain competitive within a rapidly evolving marketplace. In this regard, organizations must aspire to be more competitive than their competitors by adopting digitalization. Otherwise, they are obsolete in the digital age. Like it or not, digital transformation is not a static phenomenon; rather, it is a dynamic process. It requires organizations to adapt and evolve in response to changing technological trends, customer preferences, and market conditions. While the essence of digital transformation lies in its transformative potential to revolutionize how organizations operate, engage with customers, and create value; the power of digitalization lies in the facilities it can offer to organizations to unlock new opportunities, drive innovation, and position themselves for success within an increasingly digitalized world.

2. COMPONENTS OF DIGITAL TRANSFORMATION

Digital transformation is an in-thing and the components involve a range of technological, cultural, and strategic elements that are crucial for businesses to thrive in a digital age. In the world of the SMEs, digital transformation can enable them to remain competitive. The adoption of Internet of Things (IoT), the reengineering of business processes, and the fostering of a digital culture within the organization are components that drive transformation in organizations (Hokmabadi et al., 2024). The following section discusses the core components of digital transformation to enhance the reader's understanding.

2.1. Core Components of Digital Transformation for SMEs

The core components for driving digital transformation among SMEs are clear digital strategy and leadership. A robust technological infrastructure, particularly the utilization of internet and e-commerce platforms, offers SMEs more opportunities to expand their market reach and fortify their competitive edge (Abdul et al., 2021). The internet acts as a gateway for SMEs to transcend geographical boundaries, and to access global audiences, a feat that was previously unattainable through traditional brick-and-mortar operations. This gateway enables SMEs to promote products and services to a wider customer base, thereby allowing SMEs to diversify their revenue streams as well as reduce local market dependencies (Mokhtar et al., 2020). E-commerce platforms, on the other hand, strengthen these capabilities by providing SMEs with cost-effective solutions for setting up virtual storefronts, managing secure transactions, systematically delivering products, and managing inventories. This digital infrastructure facilitates customer interactions and transactions as well as endows SMEs with the competitive edge to compete with larger enterprises.

Further to that, the use of data and analytics to gain insights into customer behaviour, market trends, and operational performance can facilitate decision-making. Customers' experiences with a particular product or service are important as the experiences can gauge their satisfaction and loyalty. Based on customers' experiences, new ideas about the products or services can thus be extended to customers. This continuous improvement is essential for long-term success in the rapidly emerging digital economy.

It is also critical that SMEs develop the necessary skills and capabilities that can support digital transformation capabilities. This means upskilling existing employees while making initiatives in identifying new talents and recruiting them. In other words, continuous learning and development are essential for a workforce to remain competitive in the digital age (Abdullah et al., 2020). After discussing the core components of digital transformation for SMEs, the next section will discuss the Malaysian SME landscape to provide a thorough understanding of the various categories of SME structures.

3. UNDERSTANDING THE MALAYSIAN SME LANDSCAPE

The Organization for Economic Cooperation and Development (OECD) disseminated a policy brief in 2017. This policy brief underscores the lack of a globally standardized definition for SMEs. The vagueness was further compounded by the diversity seen in regulatory frameworks for SMEs across nations where the different legal and policy landscapes of the respective countries had led to the different criteria set up for categorizing businesses within the SME sector.

To a certain extent, Malaysian SMEs fare better. SME classifications adhere to a more specific set of criteria which has been stipulated by SME Corporation Malaysia. This national corporation had classified SMEs into two primary categories based on metrics that are related to the number of employees and total annual revenue. The differentiation is particularly pronounced between manufacturing firms and service-oriented enterprises. In the case of manufacturing firms, it is necessary that they have an annual sale of below RM50 million while also maintaining a workforce that is fewer than 200 full-time employees. The dual criteria set is essential for encapsulating both the financial scale of the business and its human resource capacity (SME Corp. Malaysia, 2021a, 2021b). These criteria reflect an acknowledgement of the different operational scales that characterize manufacturing enterprises within the Malaysian economic landscape.

Apart from the above, categorization of the service-oriented SMEs in Malaysia is contingent on a slightly distinct set of metrics. Specifically, service firms are considered SMEs if their annual sales do not surpass RM20 million, and if they employ fewer than 75 full-time workers. The classification considers the unique operational dynamics, and revenue structures that are characteristic of service-oriented enterprises; it acknowledges the service firms' distinct economic contributions, and market dynamics compared to other manufacturing counterparts.

In Malaysia, SMEs are demarcated based on the number of employees and annual revenue. This practical framework was created to align with the intricacies of the country's economic landscape. It facilitates a more targeted approach in supporting and regulating businesses within the SME sector. The approach is pragmatic as it acknowledges the diversity of enterprises that are operating within the Malaysian economy. Most of Malaysia's SMEs, as reported by the World Bank Group (2022), are essential to the country's economy due to their ability to boost gross domestic product (GDP), generate employment opportunities, and promote exports. The Malaysian government has implemented a range of strategies and policies as outlined in the Second Malaysia Plan (1971–1975), the Third Malaysia Plan (1976–1980), and the Fourth Malaysia Plan (1981–1985) which were aimed at supporting the SMEs. Focussing on SMEs, these initiatives were designed to bolster the industry by expanding Bumiputera entrepreneurship, stimulating employment and production rates, reducing wealth gap within the nation, and promoting equilibrium between business and industrial activities.

About 97.2% of all business entities in Malaysia are SMEs (including microenterprises). This accounts for 13.5% of all exports, 48% of the GDP, and 48% of unemployment (Department of Statistics Malaysia, 2020b). Based on the World Bank Group (2022), Malaysian SMEs experienced a steady expansion before 2020. The statistics indicated that SMEs had increased by 6.2% in 2018 and by 5.8% in 2019. These growth rates were significantly higher than both the national GDP growth rate and the GDP growth rate for non-SMEs. SMEs evidently play a crucial role in contributing to the GDP as SMEs are substantial for job creations; they contribute to the local communities and the region's economy besides supporting local suppliers and community development.

4. DIGITAL TRANSFORMATION – TRENDS AND INITIATIVES FOR MALAYSIAN SMEs

Digitalization is defined as 'the use of cutting-edge digital technologies to transform a business model and provide new revenue and value-generating opportunities' (Gartner, 2023). Businesses need to invest in new and digitally enabled strategies and models as the world progresses in order to meet the market demand. Digitalization can create 'unpredictable opportunities' and offer businesses the ability to innovate new models, products, and services. As digitization is a key driver of productivity growth and, in turn, wage growth, these disparities have led to a widening inequality between individuals, regions, and businesses. There are numerous studies on digital transformation in general, but not much has been researched on the digital transformation of Malaysian SMEs.

In the context of Malaysia, SMEs are vital to the economy. Thus, they need to undergo digital transformation based on the dynamic nature of the globalized digital economy. Digital transformation is a pervasive process that involves comprehensive organizational changes which can ultimately develop novel business models for the company or industry (Hasan et al., 2022; Kane et al., 2015; Pagani & Pardo, 2017). In the view of Teece (2010), a business model is the manifestation of 'how a company creates and delivers value to customers and then converts the payments received into profits'.

Digital transformation instigates companies to incorporate new business models through innovative business logic, for the purpose of generating greater values (Ammeran et al., 2023; Pagani & Pardo, 2017). Its application could affect the entire organizational structure. It transcends mere digitalization which involves altering basic organizational processes and tasks. Instead, digital transformation orchestrates a restructuring of processes that modifies the business logic of a firm (Li et al., 2018) or its value creation process (Gölzer & Fritzsche, 2017).

The transformative use of Information Technology (IT) induces fundamental alterations to existing business processes, routines, and capabilities. It allows healthcare providers, for instance, to enter new markets or to exit current ones (Li et al., 2018). Digital transformation also leverages on digital technologies to facilitate interactions across borders with suppliers, customers, and competitors (Singh et al., 2020). To date, the local government has even introduced several initiatives and support systems specifically aimed at assisting SMEs in the digital transformation process. These efforts include training programmes, and funding opportunities to facilitate the implementation of new technologies and to improve the overall operational efficiency (Economic Planning Unit, 2020). All these show that advancements in e-commerce, data analytics, and business intelligence contribute to the transformation of SMEs in Malaysia.

4.1. Government Initiatives and Support

The Department of Statistics Malaysia (2021) indicates that the Malaysian government encourages digital transition which was most evident during the COVID-19 pandemic. Currently, the government has introduced several initiatives and strategies.

One of the strategic plans initiated to manage the economic challenges during the COVID-19 pandemic was the *Penjana* Economic Stimulus Package (Muhamad Khair et al., 2021). Introduced in June 2020, its main objective was to stimulate economic recovery by means of supporting businesses, reducing unemployment rate, and bolstering the key sectors of economy. The *Penjana* Economic Stimulus Package also aimed to implement various initiatives and measures across multiple sectors such as providing wage subsidies, hiring incentives, and reskilling employment programmes. Thus far, a total of 124,526 individuals had participated in the reskilling and upskilling programme provided by several ministries and agencies (Department of Statistics Malaysia, 2020b). In addition, the *Penjana* Economic Stimulus Package also offers financial assistance and support to businesses such as SMEs. One of its key strategies was the SME Digitalization Grant which provides eligible SMEs with grants up to RM5000 as incentive to adopt digital technologies. The objective is to enable SMEs to equip their online presence and to expand their digital capabilities (MyGovernment, 2024). This grant can be utilized by SMEs to purchase digital tools and solutions that build or support the e-commerce platforms, digital payment systems, as well as online marketing initiatives.

Another initiative is the *TEKUN* Business Recovery Scheme (TBRS) which is a financial programme offered by *TEKUN* National, an agency under the Ministry of Agriculture and Food Industries. This scheme supports SMEs with financial aids including SME digitalization grants as a means to encourage SMEs to adopt digital technologies and automation via tax incentives and investment loans. The Department of Statistics Malaysia (2020a, October) recorded a total of 13,675 SMEs that had received RM90.6 million under this *TEKUN* scheme. Needless to say, this programme plays a significant role in supporting businesses in Malaysia as it continuously aims to address the needs of microbusinesses and SMEs effectively.

Apart from the above schemes, the Malaysian government also allocated RM150 million for Shop Malaysia Online as an e-commerce initiative that encourages consumers to shop on the e-commerce platform. The National Digital Networking Plan (Jendela) was introduced by the government to integrate the nation into the digital world. The plan aims to support the digital transformation of SMEs and microbusinesses by upgrading the internet infrastructure, network capacities, and broadband accesses in urban and rural areas. This strategic initiative aims to upsurge consumer spending with local online sellers, apart from enabling the labour market to meet a gradual regain in 2021 (Department of Statistics Malaysia, 2020b; Economic Planning Unit, 2020).

As classified in the Malaysia Digital Industry Report (MDIR), there are three industry clusters: Information Technology (INFOTECH), Digital Creative Content (DCC), and Global Business Services (GBS) (Malaysia Digital Economy Corporation (MDEC), 2023).

Based on the MDIR report, the digital economy growth rate of Malaysia has increased after the COVID-19 pandemic. This is more evident in the SME establishment as seen in the annual percentage change of the micro and small and medium enterprises' performance.

During the Movement Control Order (MCO) period in 2020, the export growth of registered SMEs had reported a decline of 33.1% or RM117.8 billion. There was around 62.1% and 3.6% decline in the services sector and the manufacturing sector, respectively. Although the agricultural sector experienced an increment of 2.6%, there was a dramatic drop in 2020. After various strategies and plans were proposed by the Malaysian government, there was about 17.8% increment in the agriculture sector, and a 20.1% growth in the manufacturing sector followed by an almost 40% increase in the services sector. As of June 2022, there were about 188,216 job creations. This statistic is 106% higher than the performance of 2021. In addition, RM40.6 billion of revenue was reported. This value notes a 65% higher increase than that of 2021. These values aligned with the investment of the digital companies which amounted to about RM25.3 billion investment in 2022 (MDEC, 2023).

4.2. E-commerce

The prominence of social media, big data, online service providers, and online platforms has had an impact on the business models utilized in the digital economy. Technology has certainly accelerated innovation across many industries; it also helped to revolutionize and disrupt established organizations, making it crucial for incumbents to quickly pick up new digital skills. E-commerce is one of the most successful achievements of digital transformation (Kumar & Ayedee, 2021). It is the equivalence to electronic commerce or e-business (Ghamdi et al., 2014). However, Damanpour and Gopalakrishnan (2001) termed e-commerce as a 'networked' business activity that creates value but exploits market opportunities by changing internal and external relationship; it is driven by the new rules of the network economy. Laudon and Laudon (2009) also noted that e-commerce serves as a subset of e-business that supports profitable business relationships and creates effective external interactions with customers and suppliers. Nonetheless, Jain et al. (2021) described e-commerce as a system with transactional goals, including search, evaluation, and post-transaction interaction; it is supported and driven by information and communication technology. It appears thus that e-commerce is normally implemented for enterprises to survive within an emerging and competitive market made up of digital transformation. Thus, enterprises need to pay attention to the significant impact of compatibility, external support, and pressure experienced when adopting the concept of e-commerce.

The outbreak of the COVID-19 pandemic in 2019 marked a major turning point for businesses around the world as the former had inevitably forced the latter to adapt to the new environment for survival. One of the most notable changes was the accelerated adoption of e-commerce as businesses sought new ways to reach customers and maintain operations. During this period, the traditional brick-and-mortar stores faced unprecedented challenges due to lockdowns, social distancing measures, and reduced foot traffic. To overcome these challenges posed by the pandemic, many businesses turned to online platforms as a measure to maintain their customer base and to generate revenue. Today, e-commerce is no longer a supplementary channel but is an important tool for business survival and development.

E-commerce adoption in the Malaysian context was primarily influenced by two types of SMEs: click-and-go and pure-play players. Click-and-go SMEs leveraged their existing physical presence while expanding into the digital marketplace to provide customers with a seamless shopping experience. The pure-play SMEs operated purely on online benefits derived from lower overhead costs, and the wider reach of audience. Some of the factors driving e-commerce adoption in Malaysia include performance expectations, employees' effort expectations, and enabling environment of government incentives and technological infrastructure. These factors enabled businesses to thrive in the digital marketplace during and after the pandemic (Keong & Anwar, 2020).

4.3. Data Analytics and Business Intelligence

Other essential tools that were needed to support digital transformation for SMEs include data analytics and business intelligence. Leveraging the data analytics and big data analytics can help SMEs to gain information about customer behaviour (such as buying patterns and sentiments), market trends (e.g. short, intermediate, and long-term trends) as well as operational performances (such as employee productivity, employee absenteeism rate, overtime hours, inventory turnover, operational expenses, etc.).

As SMEs strived to improve operational efficiency and to gain a competitive advantage, they also need to heed the integration of the technologies which are essential for informed decision-making and strategic planning. The advantage of data analytics and business intelligence for SMEs is the enhancement of decision-making capabilities. Traditionally, decision-making in business has relied on experiences and intuitions which can lead to a subjective and error-prone conclusion. With the access to data analytics that encompass statistical analysis, data mining, and predictive modelling, SMEs are thus better informed to make decisions. In line with that, business intelligence offers SMEs a timely and well-informed analysis that is generated from the data of past experiences and various other sources. In fact, data analytics can also help businesses adapt to the new breed of consumers by delivering personalized promotions for the right products at the right time, and in the customer's preferred method, thereby motivating purchases. By having data that enabled them to understand customer behaviours, businesses can therefore retain their current customers as well as attract additional customers. The data-driven approach is also expected to contribute towards the identification of further risks and potential frauds.

Customer experience in a product or service is important as a reference to the business to retain and/or to foster sales growth. By analysing the data generated from various customer platforms, such as e-commerce platforms, and customer service interactions, businesses can gain better insights into customer needs, preferences, and attitudes. Such insights provide SMEs the opportunity to tailor their marketing strategies which can help to improve customer services as well as personalize customer experience. For example, a recommendation system can suggest products to customers based on their past purchases or based on their habits and preferences. These generated suggestions can amplify customer satisfaction, thereby driving higher sales.

Customer relationship management (CRM) is one of the tools that can analyse customer data used to develop discernments for future sales so as to facilitate organizations in making better decisions. Thus far, CRM has been implemented by PERODUA, the second biggest automobile manufacturer after PROTON, to handle its interactions with both present and future clients. Statistics indicate that PERODUA had reported a 330,000 sales volume in 2023 (Statistita, 2024). The high sales volume had compelled businesses to implement a systematic approach to monitor their customers. This CRM is able to gather information from a variety of communication channels, including the company's website, phones, mobile apps, fax devices for feedback, emails, social media, and also marketing materials. The purpose of this data collection and data analytics is for the company to gain better perspectives into customer behaviour so as to retain customers through monitoring and follow-up services. Furthermore, the CRM system's business intelligence tools can present the required information through enlightening and persuasive visuals like graphs, charts, and reports all of which can help the organization to make decisions. These features which enable businesses to gather and analyse current marketing trends and sales data help companies to establish and sustain enduring customer relationships which in turn, boosts revenue (Rosely, 2018).

5. KEY TRENDS SHAPING THE DIGITAL TRANSFORMATION JOURNEY FOR MALAYSIAN SMEs

Without an iota of doubt, digital transformation has emerged as a pivotal force in reshaping the business landscapes across the globe today. This paradigm shift requires the integration of advanced digital technologies into various facts of SME operations, with profound implications for their competitiveness, innovation capacity, and market. The Organization for Economic Co-operation and Development (OECD, 2021) had noted that more than

50% of the employees in the SMEs have internet access which means that they are aware of the current trend. Further to this, Fraccastoro et al. (2021) mentioned that digital tools bring significant benefits to the firms, for example, they reduce transaction costs by providing quick access to information; they also enhance communications between suppliers, staff, and networks. This implies that there would be speedy interactions among the parties concerned. To add to this, Ulas (2019) also indicated that digital transformation in SMEs should not only focus on the technical parts like software–hardware updates, but also the adaptation of the institutional and operational ecosystem. This offers a wider and far reaching circuit to business.

Nonetheless, there are several empirical studies on employee complete breaks and the impact of new technology that had gathered some evidence of up/reskilling and deskilling incidents because of technological change (Adepoju & Aigbavboa, 2021; Jones et al., 2014; Zimmermann, 2016). Clearly, technology bears practical implications not just on the types of jobs accessible, but also on how people live and work as evidenced by the rise of 'flexible' and remote working trends (Li, 2022). Meantime, Brunetti et al. (2020) had emphasized on the importance of digital education, digital culture, and talent. They noted that digital education is crucial for training students to master the logical and computational skills as well as the ethics of using internet as electronic devices in the early stage of usage. This aspect is important because it is related to the downside of technology such as using it to spread fake news, to cyberbully, financial frauds, and other kinds of dishonesty. The advent of technology has placed SMEs to confront themselves with an array of unprecedented challenges as well as remarkable opportunities. This dynamic landscape is further compounded by the rapid advancement of digital technology, notably in the context of IR 4.0.

IR 4.0 was first introduced in the year 2011 in Germany (Bartevyan, 2015). The concept emphasizes industrial manufacturing via digitalization and the exploitation of the potentials of new technologies (Rojko, 2017). IR 4.0 transformative technologies include the IoT, artificial intelligence, cloud computing, and big data analytics, tools which can enable SMEs to streamline their operations as well as partake in better informed decision-making processes (Janssen et al., 2021; Lee et al., 2019). It was also noted by Ahn et al. (2021) that the integration of digital technology within SMEs can increase productivity, reduce operation costs, and achieve personal customer demands through connectivity and collaborations between SMEs and stakeholders in the context of enabling real-time communication and data sharing activities. By leveraging the opportunities afforded by IR 4.0, SMEs can drive innovation, competitiveness, and sustainable growth in the digital era.

6. CHAPTER SUMMARY

This chapter has explored the role that digital transformation plays in the growth and competitiveness of Malaysian SMEs. It commenced by discussing why digital transformation is crucial for businesses; it also emphasized on how it can improve customer experiences as well as foster innovations. This chapter also highlighted the necessity of digital transformation within the SME landscape for the purpose of retaining their competitiveness upon a digital platform which also serves as the marketplace. The components of digital transformation were discussed in details which encompass technological, cultural, and strategic elements all of which are essential for modern businesses. The key components include a clear digital strategy, robust technological infrastructure, integration of digital tools and platforms, and the focus on customer experience and engagement. They are important for SMEs that wish to thrive in the digital age.

The chapter then delved into the core components of digital transformation specifically for SMEs. The discussion of government initiatives and support, e-commerce, data analytics, and CRM system were also presented. The Malaysian SME landscape was also highlighted. The chapter also examined current digital transformation trends and initiatives occurring among Malaysian SMEs. The discussion covered government support and initiatives, and industry collaboration. Other aspects of digital transformation such as the acceleration of e-commerce, the importance of data analytics, and the adoption of advanced technologies were also explored. This chapter serves as a comprehensive guide for Malaysian SMEs on how to navigate digital transformation by emphasizing on the importance of strategic planning, technological adoption, and continuous innovation for sustainable growth and competitiveness in the digital economy.

Clearly, digital transformation is important for SMEs if they wish to remain relevant and competitive within the rapidly evolving business landscape. By embracing innovative digital technologies in the enterprise, SMEs can unlock new opportunities for growth, reshape their business models by expanding the market, enhance their operational efficiency, as well as improve customer engagement.

REFERENCES

Abdul, M. H., Alias, R. A., & Tapsir, S. (2021). Digital transformation and SMEs: Challenges and policy implications. *International Journal of Innovation, Creativity and Change*, 14(2), 427–443.

Abdullah, N. A., Muhamad, R., & Ab Talib, M. S. (2020). Digital technology adoption among Malaysian small and medium enterprises (SMEs): The role of human capital. *International Journal of Human Capital and Information Technology Professionals*, *11*(3), 1–16.

Adepoju, O. O., & Aigbavboa, C. O. (2021). Assessing knowledge and skills gap for construction 4.0 in a developing economy. *Journal of Public Affairs*, *21*(3), e2264.

Ahn, J. H., Lee, J., & Kim, H. (2021). The impact of Industry 4.0 on organizational innovation and firm performance: The moderating roles of dynamic capabilities and organizational learning. *Technological Forecasting and Social Change*, *169*, 120785.

Ammeran, M. Y., Noor S., & Yusof, M. (2023). Digital transformation of Malaysian small and medium-sized enterprises: A review and research direction. In B. Alareeni & A. Hamdan (Eds.), *Innovation of businesses, and digitalization during Covid-19 pandemic* (pp. 255–278). Springer. https://doi.org/10.1007/978-3-031-08090-6_16

Bartevyan, L. (2015). *Industry 4.0 – Summary report*. DLG e.V.

Brunetti, F., Matt, D. T., Bonfanti, A., De Longhi, A., Pedrini, G., & Orzes, G. (2020). Digital transformation challenges: Strategies emerging from a multi-stakeholder approach. *The TQM Journal*, *32*(4), 1754–2732.

Cao, K., Xu, Y., Wu, Q., Wang, J., & Liu, C. (2021). Optimal channel and logistics service selection strategies in the e-commerce context. *Electronic Commerce Research and Applications*, *48*, 101070.

Damanpour, F., & Gopalakrishnan, S. (2001). The dynamics of the adoption of product and process innovations in organizations. *Journal of Management Studies*, *38*, 45–65.

Department of Statistics Malaysia. (2020a, October). *Key statistics of labour force in Malaysia*. https://v1.dosm.gov.my/v1/index.php?r=column/cthemeByCat&cat=124&bul_id=WVJTenlQKzdzUDRYNFJqUE1BWWVIZz09&menu_id=Tm8zcnRjdVRNWWlpWjRlbmtlaDk1UT09

Department of Statistics Malaysia. (2020b). *Small and medium enterprises (SMEs) performance 2020*. Department of Statistics Malaysia. https://www.dosm.gov.my/v1/index.php?r=column/cthemeByCat&cat=159&bul_id=KzdrS25pRTZ1VGFkcTlNY0FEczBYUT09&menu_id=TE5CRUZCblh4ZTZMODZIbmk2aWRRQT09#:~:text=The%20share%20of%20SMEs%20employment,2019%20(7.32%20million%20persons

Department of Statistics Malaysia. (2021). *Micro, small & medium enterprises (MSMEs) performance.* https://www.dosm.gov.my/portal-main/release-content/micro-small-&-medium-enterprises-msmes-performance-2021

Economic Planning Unit. (2020). *Malaysia digital economy blueprint.* https://www.ekonomi.gov.my/sites/default/files/2021-02/malaysia-digital-economy-blueprint.pdf

Fraccastoro, S., Gabrielsson, M., & Pullins, E. B. (2021). The integrated use of social media, digital, and traditional communication tools in the B2B sales process of international SMEs. *International Business Review, 15* (4), 101776.

Gartner. (2023). *Digitalization.* https://www.gartner.com/en/information-technology/glossary/digitalization#:~:text=Digitalization%20is%20the%20use%20of,moving%20to%20a%20digital%20business

Ghamdi, R., Alfarraj, O., & Bahaddad, A. (2014). How retailers at different stages of e-commerce maturity evaluate their entry to e-commerce activities? *Journal of Computer Science and Information Technology*, 2(2), 37–71.

Gölzer, P., & Fritzsche, A. (2017). Data-driven operations management: Organisational implications of the digital transformation in industrial practice. *Production Planning & Control, 28*(16), 1332–1343. https://doi.org/10.1080/09537287.2017.1375148

Hasan, N. A., Rahim, M. A., Ahmad, S. H., & Meliza, M. (2022). Digitalization of business for small and medium-sized enterprises (SMEs). *Environment Behaviour Proceedings Journal*, 7(19), 11–16. https://doi.org/10.21834/ebpj.v7i19.3270

Hokmabadi, H., Rezvani, S. M. H. S., & de Matos, C. A. (2024). Business resilience for small and medium enterprises and startups by digital transformation and the role of marketing capabilities—A systematic review. *Systems*, 12(6), 220.

Jain, V., Malviya, B., & Arya, S. (2021). An overview of electronic commerce (e-commerce). *Journal of Contemporary Issues in Business and Government*, 27(3), 665–670.

Janssen, M., Wimmer, M. A., & Deljoo, A. (2021). Editorial: Smart government in a smart world: Digitalization, digital transformation, and beyond. *Frontiers in Blockchain*, 4, 43.

Jones, P., Simmons, G., Packham, G., Beynon-Davies, P., & Pickernell, D. (2014). An exploration of the attitudes and strategic responses of sole-proprietor microenterprises in adopting information and communication technology. *International Small Business Journal, 32*(3), 285–306. https://doi.org/10.1177/0266242612461802

Kane, G. C., Palmer, D., Kiron, D., & Buckley, N. (2015). Strategy, not technology, drives digital transformation: Becoming a digitally mature enterprise. *MIT Sloan Management Review*. https://sloanreview.mit.edu/projects/strategy-drives-digital-transformation/

Keong, H., & Anwar, F. (2020). Malaysian SMEs performance and the use of E-Commerce: A multi-group analysis of click-and-mortar and pure-play E-Retailers. *Pakistan Journal of Commerce and Social Sciences, 14*(1), 1–33.

Kumar, A., & Ayedee, N. (2021). Technology adoption: A solution for SMEs to overcome problems during Covid-19. *Academy of Marketing Studies Journal, 25*(1), 1–16. https://papers.ssrn.com/sol3/papers.cfm?abstract_id=3745814

Laudon, K., & Laudon, J. (2009). *Management information systems* (11th ed.). Prentice Hall.

Lee, J., Bagheri, B., & Kao, H. A. (2019). A cyber-physical systems architecture for industry 4.0-based manufacturing systems. *Manufacturing Letters, 19*, 1–5.

Li, L. (2022). Reskilling and upskilling the future-ready workforce for Industry 4.0 and beyond. *Information Systems Frontiers, 13*, 1–16. https://doi.org/10.1007/s10796-022-10308-y

Li, L., Su, F., Zhang, W., & Mao, J. Y. (2018). Digital transformation by SME entrepreneurs: A capability perspective. *Information Systems Journal, 28*(6), 1129–1157.

Malaysia Digital Economy Corporation (MDEC). (2023). *Malaysia Digital Industry Report 2021-H1 2022: A comparative analysis*. https://mdec.my/static/pdf/publication/Malaysia%20Digital%20Industry%20Report_2021-H1%202022%20ver%2023.pdf

Mokhtar, M. M., Tan, W. L., & Lee, V. H. (2020). Overcoming resistance to change in small and medium enterprises (SMEs) digital transformation initiatives: A conceptual framework. *International Journal of Academic Research in Business and Social Sciences, 10*(9), 1262–1278.

Muhamad Khair, N. K., Lee, K. E., & Mokhtar, M. (2021). Community-based monitoring in the new normal: A strategy for tackling the COVID-19 pandemic in Malaysia. *International Journal of Environmental Research and Public Health*, *18*, 6712. https://doi.org/10.3390/ijerph18136712

MyGovernment. (2024). *Short-term economic recovery plan (PENJANA)*. https://www.malaysia.gov.my/portal/content/31148

Organization for Economic Co-operation and Development (OECD). (2021). *The global recovery is strong but imbalanced*. https://www.oecd.org/economic-outlook/december-2021/

Pagani, M., & Pardo, C. (2017). The impact of digital technology on relationships in a business network. *Industrial Marketing Management*, 67, 185–192.

Phoong, S. W., Phoong, S. Y., & Ho, S. T. (2022). Technology, organisation and environment factor on mobile payment implementation: Focus on SMEs in Malaysia. *International Journal of Mobile Communications*, *20*(5), 519–540.

Phoong, S. W., Phoong, S. Y., Moghavvemi, S., & Sulaiman, A. (2020). Measuring the influence of hedonic value, social presence and teaching presence on students' cognitive presence through the implementation of the smart classroom. *International Journal of Learning Technology*, *15*(2), 130–149.

Rojko, A. (2017). Industry 4.0 concept: Background and overview. *Special Focus Paper Interactive Mobile Technologies, 11*(5), 77–90.

Rosely, S. (2018, December 26). *Customer relation management (CRM) system at PERODUA*. Prezi Inc. https://prezi.com/p/eczlnunveoo2/business-information-system/

Šaković Jovanović, J., Vujadinović, R., Mitreva, E., Fragassa, C., & Vujović, A. (2020). The relationship between e-commerce and firm performance: The mediating role of internet sales channels. *Sustainability*, *12*, 6993. https://doi.org/10.3390/su12176993

Singh, A., Klarner, P., & Hess, T. (2020). How do chief digital officers pursue digital transformation activities? The role of organization design parameters. *Long Range Planning*, *53*(3), 101890.

SME Corp. Malaysia. (2021a). *Guidelines for new SME definition*. Retrieved October 2, 2018, from http://www.smecorp.gov.my/index.php/en/policies/2015-12-21-09-09-49/sme-definition

SME Corp. Malaysia. (2021b). *SME definitions*. https://www.smecorp.gov.my/index.php/en/policies/2020-02-11-08-01-24/sme-definition

Statistita. (2024, February 9). *Leading car manufacturers in Malaysia in 2023, by sales volume.* https://www.statista.com/statistics/516276/passenger-vehicle-sales-in-malaysia-by-brand/#:~:text=In%202023%2C%20the%20Malaysian%20car,sales%20of%20over%20150%2C000%20cars

Teece, D. (2010). Business models, business strategy and innovation. *Long Range Planning*, *43*(2–3), 172–194.

Ulas, D. (2019). Digital transformation process and SMEs. *Procedia Computer Science*, *158*, 662–671.

Wang, X., Wong, Y. D., Teo, C. C., Yuen, K. F. & Feng, X. (2020). The four facets of self-collection service for e-commerce delivery: Conceptualisation and latent class analysis of user segments. *Electronic Commerce Research and Applications*, *39*, 100896.

World Bank Group. (2022). *Malaysian SME programme efficiency review.* https://documents1.worldbank.org/curated/en/099255003152238688/pdf/P17014606709a70f50856d0799328fb7040.pdf

Zimmermann, D. V. (2016). SMEs and digitalisation: The current position, recent developments and challenges. *KfW Research*, *138*, 1–7. https://www.kfw.de/PDF/Download-Center/Konzernthemen/Research/PDFDokumente-Fokus-Volkswirtschaft/Fokus-englische-Dateien/Fokus-Nr.-138-August-2016-Digitalisierung_EN.pdf

2

THE IMPORTANCE OF SME's DIGITAL TRANSFORMATION IN PROMOTING THE MALAYSIAN ECONOMY

ABSTRACT

Small and medium enterprises (SMEs) contribute to the Malaysian economic indicators, such as the gross domestic Product (GDP) by producing goods and services, generating exports to expand the market, and creating job opportunities for employment. Following the Industrial Revolution 4.0 (IR 4.0), various technologies, such as artificial intelligence (AI), robotics, cloud computing, big data, and the internet of things (IoT) have been used in SMEs' operations and productions. This leads to the process of digital transformation which in turn enables SMEs and all economic sectors apply more sophisticated technologies that can lead to innovations and new business models. Digitalization through the IR 4.0 technologies could increase people's interactions, facilitate economic transactions, and change consumer consumption habits while stimulating new consumer demands. Businesses conducted through digitalization can be beneficial to both the supply side and the demand side of the economy, thereby accelerating the economic growth of the country. From the supply end, digitalization enhances workers' productivity and production growth. It enables mass production of goods and services, reduces operations and production costs, and increases investment returns. From the demand side, digitalization provides the market platform with bigger interactions from business to customers (B2C), in terms of cataloguing, pricing, ordering, transfer payment, delivery tracking, and after sales service gained from features, such as customer reviews and refund matters. Digitalization can also create new task-delivery approaches, and job market landscapes for both the formal and informal sectors of business. In short, digital transformation can create a dynamic relationship between supply, demand, and the enablers. This would ultimately contribute to the economic growth of Malaysia.

Keywords: Digital transformation; demand and supply; SME; efficiency; economic growth

1. INTRODUCTION

SMEs play an important role in the Malaysian economy. They contribute to the Malaysian GDP by producing goods and services, generating exports to expand the market, and creating job opportunities for employment. Following the IR 4.0 and its advancements, many businesses have learnt to use the technologies that come with it, such as AI, cloud computing, big data, and the IoT. They are used by SMEs to conduct their operations and to expand their productions. This chapter aims to uncover how SMEs' digital transformation can enhance the Malaysian economy. As has been said, digitalization using the IR 4.0 technology can enhance workers' productivity and businesses' production. This technology enables businesses to induce mass production which is good for sales. However, the firms involved would require highly skilled labour and qualified innovators who are equipped with the expertise to handle, manage, and expand on their digitalization process.

2. UNDERSTANDING THE IMPACT OF DIGITAL TRANSFORMATION ON MALAYSIAN ECONOMY

Digital transformation is the portmanteau of digital computing and economy whereby traditional brick-and-mortar economic activities, such as production, distribution, and trade, are being transformed by the World Wide Web technologies, and the Internet. Digital transformation involves various tools like the Internet, mobile technology, big data, special devices, and personal consumer data, and it is performed through various processes which involve multiple sectors. Digital transformation is reliant on the information and communications technology. The economic activities that emerged from such technology can then be used to connect the individuals with various businesses for multiple functions and operations.

Tsao and Chang (2010) stated that physical stores are no longer the main attraction for consumers since online shopping became popular. This is because online shopping offers consumers a wide variety of products, the convenience of searching for different products, the accessibility of quick transactions, and the provision of individualized service information. With the rapid emergence of the IR 4.0, most of the businesses in Malaysia have come to realize that the advancement of digital technology is rapid and ever evolving, and given the failure to become a part of this revolution, they would be unable to sustain their growth which can greatly affect their business revenues. Nonetheless, there is a need to understand the implications of the business revenues created by social media following the IR 4.0 which has become the power of social media and digital technologies today.

2.1. Digital Transformation Eases the Economic Transactions

Malaysia's economic growth is rapidly changing due to the adoption of digital technologies. The country is witnessing a swift digital transformation that is changing the way businesses are operating. People interactions, economic transactions, and consumer behaviour are changing due to the accessibility of the vast digital ecosystems. Inevitably, businesses are becoming involved with the digital transformation being discussed due to the latter's benefits. For instance, digital transformation improves consumer interactions as well as business operations (Berman, 2012).

One of the most important elements in digital technology is the digital platform it offers users for connections, such as Facebook and Alibaba. These are widely used by consumers because they support transactions which are both convenient and easy for the users. In online shopping, whether for goods or services, consumers prefer interactions on accessible platforms. Social media platforms offer consumers artificial conversation threads that are supported by chatbots to help them solve some of their enquiries and needs. Sellers could then take over the conversation when there is a need. Otherwise, the basic problematic questions and processes such as ordering, and payment are easily resolved by chatbots. This makes it convenient for customers and marketers since the need for call centres and friction in customer service can be significantly reduced (Kaplan & Haenlein, 2019).

Digitalization facilitates transactions via mobile wallets, also known as electronic wallet (e-wallet). This application allows users to pay and receive money conveniently using either their mobile phones, tablets, or smart watches, without the need for cash. Users only need to save their debit and credit card information in their mobile wallet which is linked directly to their bank accounts (George & Sunny, 2021). Accordingly, users can top up their mobile wallet through bank cards or through online transfers at any time and in any place. Mobile wallets are also secure because it is more difficult to steal mobile wallets even though the user's phone has been stolen, unlike actual debit cards or credit cards. The reason for the difficulties is that mobile wallets have encryption keys that might not reveal any important information. In addition, mobile wallets also allow users to shop online and pay various bills such as parking fees, movie tickets, and other fees more conveniently. Features such as coupons, rewards, and points have also become the reason that attracted users to use mobile wallets.

There are three main types of mobile wallets provided by third parties. They include open wallets, closed wallets, and semi-closed wallets (*CFI Team*). Firstly, open wallets are used directly by banks or third parties. They allow users to withdraw cash out of their account, or to use money from their mobile wallets to pay for purchases. Secondly, closed wallets allow users to make payments and transactions with specific merchants. Users cannot use the funds to make transactions with other merchants, and they are not allowed to take out their cash. Thirdly, semi-closed mobile wallets allow users to use funds in the wallet to exercise transactions with merchants who have a contract with the mobile wallet company. Users cannot take out the cash, but are allowed to withdraw and transfer funds to their bank accounts. Third parties that provide e-wallet services include PayPal, Shopee Pay, Touch 'n Go e-wallet, Boost, Alipay, and more. They serve as intermediaries for banks, buyers, and sellers. They make the economic market's transaction procedures much easier and quicker.

2.2. Digital Transformation and Return on Investment

Digital technologies are driving transformative changes which have led to a shift in the economic paradigm. These new technologies are reshaping the product and factor market, and profoundly altering business and work. As technologies evolve and integrate into business manoeuvre, the investment into digital transformation for business is preferable as it serves as a driver of market growth and value. Digital transformation can save much time and energy with workflow optimization and simplicity; hence it can reduce the operational cost. The AI can imitate the human's work which in turn reduces the cost of labour. The benefits of digital transformation can reduce operational, marketing, and production costs.

While firms need to consider the high cost of adopting technological infrastructure, the mass production of output resulted by digital technology can increase more revenues and profits. More products and services can be produced and marketed with low cost of operation and production thereby enabling businesses to achieve the break-even at a shorter time. In this regard, the investment made in digital technology can gain a return after a certain period of time.

2.3. Digital Transformation and Cost Reduction

Digital transformation encourages more online business creations which can target more audiences. It incurs less investment for premise rentals, and less cost for hiring workers due to its involvement of automation and robotic technologies. Sellers involved in online businesses only need to rent or buy the platform at affordable prices instead of renting a physical business premise. In addition, the business operation conducted via online, for example, meet with clients by online meeting, simplifying the process of procurement by using electronic procurement or e-procurement, can save an operational cost. Moreover, sharing information in digital platform can increase awareness among consumers about the products and services offered by the companies. These imply that digital transformation reduces operation, marketing, and production costs. Moreover, the IoT plays a significant role in interconnecting objects to improve business manoeuvre. It can identify, integrate the identification, and also track the sensors. The IoT is expected to become an approach that saves time processing, reduces operation costs, as well as enhances the manufacturing system for higher efficiency (Anderl, 2015).

2.4. Digital Transformation and Job Creation in Formal and Informal Sectors

The dynamics of labour market, caused by scientific and technological innovations, will inevitably impact the total employment volume in Malaysia. The advancement of digitalization can lead to job creations which involve the handling of information, managing of knowledge, storing of data, and also the monitoring of programming issues (Bahri & Min, 2023) in the formal sector. Hence, it could lead to the need for more skilled labour in digital skills. Digital transformation also encourages more online platforms to be integrated for businesses with the sharing economy model. This sharing economy model is the epitome of convenience for Generation Z and the millennials (Forbes, 2019). It can create a gig economy, and generate more opportunities for gig activities in the informal sector.

Taken together, SMEs have a demand for specialized labour force, thereby also expanding employment opportunities. It seems apparent that the advancement of AI technologies would lead to the creation of new products, and the expansion of new markets, hence absorbing a portion of the unemployed workforce (Berriman & Hawksworth, 2017). When capitalists take advantage of the new values created by new products and new markets, it is also time to see a drive in investment growth and bigger job possibilities Suskind & Susskind, 2016). This means that emerging technologies can serve as a new employment mechanism because they create more work prospects (David & David, 2017).

2.5. Digital Transformation and New Work Landscapes

The implementation of the remote-work and work-online trend is witnessing a change in the work landscape due to digital transformation. This trend was more evidently seen during the COVID-19 pandemic of 2019/2020. The new work landscape in terms of communication is changing after pandemic. Many operational procedures are conducted via online. For example, online meeting with colleagues, online approval for leave, document approval with digital signature, online training, and many other procedures. Based on the experience, it can be seen that digital platforms made it easier for employers and employees to stay engaged when they worked from home. Furthermore, foreign company is able to hire skilled foreign workers from abroad by keeping them in their home country with the assistance of digital work platform. The new work landscape is not only making business operation easier but also in reducing more logistic costs.

Besides, digital technology makes it superior in the organization to have less monitoring physically at the site while doing multitask jobs. They can monitor their workers at the site with closed-circuit television (CCTV) whereby the application is installed in their mobile phone. In addition, digital transformation not only makes job easier but also improves workers' work–life balance. It allows workers to deliver their tasks at anytime and anywhere while taking care of their families. Having a better work–life balance among workers will improve their productivity and as a result enhance better outcomes for organizations and businesses.

2.6. Digital Transformation and the Economies of Scale

One important aspect of digitization is that it could achieve great economies of scale. Economies of scale are cost advantages reaped by companies when production becomes efficient. Companies can achieve economies of scale by increasing production while lowering per-unit production costs. McCulloch (1821) believed that the use of machines could greatly improve labour productivity, which would lead to a reduction in product prices, and an increase in consumption quantity, and production quantity (Bessen, 2015). In the advancement of digital transformation by using AI and IoT, the production rises faster than costs. It can reduce operational, marketing, and production costs, and at the same time increase productivity in producing products and services, which is in line with the economies of scale advantages.

2.7. Digital Business Models and Market Structure Transition

The digital economy offers three distinct business models. The first model involves directly selling digital products, such as Windows applications from Microsoft. However, companies operating under this model are not easy to enter, as they require experts in specialized fields such as programming and computer systems to innovate and keep up with the latest technology. This model is characterized by the monopoly market structure. The second model is the business model that provides products to direct users, and its revenues are derived from people's usage of its service. The third business model is the digital economy where retailers can be diversified such that the platform providers can tailor the business functions. Since there are no barriers to enter the digital platform market for certain business functions, the market structure for the second business model is thus viewed as a monopolistic competition.

Malaysians are swiftly adopting the digital technology, but they are not adopting it as a technology innovator or creator. This means that most industries in Malaysia would be applying the second business model for the purpose of conducting tasks, such as publishing the video recorded in YouTube, and then earning money from the click rates, as shown by the growing number of subscribers and viewers. This chapter recommends the use of the third business model explained in digital economy. It is the model where the business provides platform for interactions from B2C in terms of cataloguing, pricing, ordering, transferring payments, tracking delivery, and after sales service such as customer reviews and refund matters. Malaysians can also apply the third business model which involves the use of an independent contractor as a gig activist, such as Foodpanda, GrabFood, and GrabCar. By providing and offering customers with the same goods sourced from different sellers within the same catalogue, platform providers such as Lazada and Shopee, are in perfect competition via the third business model, consumers are free to choose the sellers who charge the lowest price for the same product.

2.8. Enhancing Competitiveness and the Blue Ocean Strategy

Blue ocean strategy is about creating and capturing uncontested market, whereby the firms supported each other. With the digital platforms offering an overwhelming amount of product information, customers can evaluate the quality of the products. Since digitalization can breach the asymmetric information assumption within a monopolistic competitive market, SMEs should strive to enhance their performances by competing in the market. Through this way, SMEs would not only improve their competitive advantage, but also be able to keep an attraction for their loyal and potential buyers.

Digital business is also witnessing an emerging paradigm with businesses across the board collaborating with each other. Businesses are using digital information and communication, social media, and new technology platforms to improve their business and management processes, in addition to being competitive (Costa et al., 2019). Digital platforms have become the norm, to the extent that they are offering SMEs the opportunity to internationalize, and to increase competitiveness (Costa et al., 2020). Consequently, collaborations across businesses in the sharing economy had led to the blue ocean strategy culture, where the businesses enter into an untapped market, create demand, and see opportunity for high monetary growth.

3. UNDERSTANDING NEW ECONOMIC LANDSCAPE IN DIGITALIZATION

Generation Z and the millennials are the biggest group of consumers in digital transformation. Their commonality is that they are a part of the digital revolution. Digitalization became more obvious when these groups began using smartphones to perform almost every transaction instead of using desktops and the traditional brick-and-mortar devices. Part of their daily culture is to make an order to buy a good or to conduct business transactions via smartphones (Perna, 2019). They were born with different needs, mindsets, and preferences, and they are also the demographics who had created a market with an economic landscape that was based on technology. Clearly, the advancement of digital technology and the information flow that could cross borders had made information more transparent and symmetrical, to the point that it could reach just about any market player. Digital transformation is developing rapidly, and the application of digital technology has broken down interdepartmental barriers, making the sharing of knowledge and data reality reminiscent of public goods (Wang & Shao, 2024).

With the increased usage of social media by the millennials, more businesses have also succumbed to the opportunity to promote their products and services via digital marketing. Also known as millennials, the Generation Y group plays an important role because they are vital in influencing the behaviour towards online shopping which has also increased business revenues. The Meltwater report of 2024 noted that the young generation aged between 16 and 24 is the largest population indulging in the main social media with those aged from 25 to 34 adhering more to Instagram, with 27% of males and 26% of females indulging in this platform. Based on this outcome, entrepreneurs are seeking the use of this powerful platform to strengthen their business values and to enhance their competitive edge as well as business profits (Aral & Weill, 2007).

In terms of government policy, the Malaysian Digital Economy Blueprint was launched in 2019 with the aim of targeting the contributions derived from the digital economy to aid the Malaysian growth. To transform the Malaysian economy from low-cost manufacturing to a high value competent manufacturer, the government then launched the 'IR4:Industry Forward' policy in 2021. It was targeted to strengthen and improve the manufacturing industry, and to increase productivity as well as efficiency. This policy played a crucial role in providing relevant assistance and guidance for SMEs to adopt the IR 4.0 technologies.

3.1. Inception of Digital Trade and E-commerce

The digital platforms benefitted SMEs by providing consumers with more conveniences such as shorter shipping times, wider products suited to local and international markets, and interfaces that provide greater affinity with linguistic and cultural nuances. SMEs were able to join the digital economy because of the relatively low barrier to enter the global market (UNCTAD, 2022). The digital platforms thus enabled easy trading of the digital products, such as software, videos, songs, and any digital materials, across borders.

3.2. Omni-channel Approach to Sales

Malaysia's online shopping apps such as Lazada and Shopee are adopting digital technologies such as the IoT, AI, cloud computing, and so on as a measure to maximize their productivity and profit revenues. According to Shopee's regional managing director, Ion Ho, Malaysians are better served with more conveniences now due to greater internet connectivity following IR.0 (Ismail, 2019). However, some domestic companies are still unaware that the existing market structure had transformed to become efficient production approaches. Many SMEs do not have much awareness about the advantages of technologies as the adoption of social media in business settings is relatively low (Braojos-Gomez et al., 2015; Michaelidou et al., 2011). Their restricted resources may be one of the causes preventing them to enhance their customers' outreach.

3.3. The Role of Social Media

Social media is a digital platform that provides information to the targeted audience. It is used for marketing purposes. Social media marketing is the process of creating contents for social media platforms so as to promote the products and services, to build communities with targeted audiences, and to drive traffic for business.

In this age of modern technology, social media plays a significant role in everyone's life. It is providing people with a social networking platform to engage with each other, to interact, and to access information easily (Siddiqui & Singh, 2016). It is a collection of digital software which enables the users to share their contents and information through social networks. According to the Petrosyan (2024), as of July 2024, there are 5.45 billion internet users worldwide, which is 67.1% of the global population.

In accordance with Woodward's (2024) outcome, the average daily social media usage is 2 hours and 27 minutes, and the average number of social media accounts is 6.6. Social media has had an average compounded growth rate of 12% since 2012. It has grown at an average rate of 13.5 new users every second throughout 2021. It was also noted that the world's population that is over the age of 13 uses social media in some platforms. In addition, 93% of people who use the internet regularly also used social media. In the Malaysian context, the number of social media users had increased by 4.8 million or 20% between early 2023, and the beginning of 2024. The number of social media users in Malaysia is 83.1% of the total population in 2024

(Siddharta, 2024). The adoption of social media has become an essential need in the business marketing mix (Mangold & Faulds, 2009).

According to Mark Zuckerberg, co-founder of Facebook, businesses should make it a point to understand the usage of social networking technologies (Hoffmann et al., 2018). Through the adoption of social media, businesses can approach more customers to expand their business growth (Fruhling & Digman, 2000). A myriad of benefits can be reaped from social media, and this includes building brand loyalty and public awareness because social media helps to publicize products and services throughout the world. According to a study by McKinsey consultants, 69% of respondents had stated that their marketing effectiveness had improved, their cost of business had decreased, and they witnessed more business benefits and higher revenues as a result of using social media in their businesses (Bughin et al., 2012). Manyika et al. (2013) also found that businesses benefit in terms of a reduction in time to market their product, an improvement in their partnerships, more rapid access to external knowledge, an increase in innovations, and a boost in business revenues.

Past studies (Agnihotri et al., 2016; Durkin et al., 2013; He, 2014; McCann & Barlow, 2015) had shown that the relationship between businesses and customers can become closer and more competitive through social media. New products or services can be generated through the relationship formed via the internet, and this eventually increases sales and revenues (Porter, 2001). The use of social media also helps business brands to be easily exposed to users which then generate more followers and customers.

Consumers' attention can be garnered by the advertisements posted on social networks due to curiosity and interest, and buyers can also easily search for the details of particular products or services on social media. They also have access to making inquiries to sellers almost immediately. The online discussions generated through social interactions among users on social media had also been found to positively impact business sales (Stephen & Galak, 2012; Trusov et al., 2009). Thus, when consumers' purchasing intentions increase, the business sales revenue also improves.

3.4. AI and Automation

AI is a new type of technical science that was developed based on research, theories, methods, techniques, and applied systems. It was created with the pur pose of simulating, extending, and increasing human intelligence. It has been defined as a discipline of knowledge where the science of how to represent knowledge, how to acquire it, and how to use it, are made available. AI is the study of making computers to perform intelligent tasks in which only human had the ability to accomplish; it encompasses using the law of human intelligent activities, and the construction of an artificial system that contains a certain level of intelligence. It is also a study of making computers perform jobs that previously required human intelligence to perform. Along with the IR 4.0, the concept of AI has begun entering our lives in various ways as seen through the invention of driverless cars, face recognition, machine translation, voice recognition, and intelligent customer service robots. It has brought about significant economic benefits to various businesses as well as many changes and convenience in our lives (Bilal et al., 2019).

The intelligence and advancement of networking systems are inevitable in the era of the IR 4.0 (Zhang et al., 2014). The IR 4.0 is driven by the development of physical technology, biological technology, and digital technology. Schwab (2017) noted that the world is getting more digitalized, and the enhancement of digital technology has improved innovations in every aspect. Digital technology focusses on four major aspects – the IoT, AI, and machine learning, big data, and cloud computing, besides digital platforms. Most businesses believed that digital technology has contributed to industrial manufacturing, and the development of economy. They utilized digital technologies to boost their business revenues. With the trend shifting towards online marketing, many businesses have also become interested in using social media to increase their sales and revenues. Consequently, social media has become the global marketplace and platform for businesses to be conducted online.

The country's economic growth is accelerated by the development of IR 4.0 as it could benefit the manufacturing industries while also nurturing the innovation-driven growth. The IR 4.0 has saved cost on human resources, and reduced labour time. This led to an increase in production and revenues. However, with technology, unemployment rate is also expected due to the replacement of technology. Many countries have put their efforts into production following the concept of IR 4.0. As a result, there is not only a high-tech competition between entrepreneurship, but also between countries. It appears that the IR 4.0 has created new opportunities for businesses to sustain themselves; it has also enabled businesses to overcome certain problems besides accelerating the production process by adopting innovative technologies. Following Industry 4.0, businesses like SMEs need to engage with social media by dealing with the emerging technologies in ICT (Muhammad et al., 2010). This is to ensure that the businesses could benefit from the technologies and be capable of competing in the global arena (Cova et al., 2007).

3.5. Seller and Consumer Protection in Online Transaction

The digital platform in online transactions needs additional features to enhance safety and privacy as a safeguard for both consumers and sellers. These features can be anchored by AI. To accelerate the progress of the networking technology, AI systems which resemble human thoughts and behaviour were developed. Machine learning, which is a basic part of AI, has been widely used in security market analysis, biometric fields, and other purposes. Many of the traditional tasks which required plenty of time, such as cancelling orders, and updating new products can now be enhanced by machine learning. The burden of salespeople can now be reduced with automation that offers quick processing of orders, documentation, and services.

In addition, digital technology also involves big data and cloud computing which offer specialized benefits. Big data comprises of a huge variety and volume of data which need to be cleaned and handled by cloud computing so as to make them smaller (Purcell, 2014). In this regard, manufacturing firms should attain the cloud computing technology since it can have a significant effect on organizational sustainability such that it helps to manage the value-chain ecosystem (Chang et al., 2013). Moreover, a private cloud is also available for making information more secure.

3.6. Dynamic Relationships Between Demand, Supply, and the Enablers

In today's digital economy, more products and services are supplied to more consumers with less marginal cost. The economic growth in which the rapid rise of AI, big data, and mobile internet has brought about new industries, products, services, and business models. They provide platforms offering interactions between sellers and consumers in addition to stimulating new consumer demands. Digital platforms thus act as an enabler for sellers to market their products, and for consumers to demand more business creations.

When a variety of products are offered by many sellers on the digital platform, customers have more options. Therefore, easy access to the digital platforms can create more demands in the market. Digitalization in marketing offers businesses a greater extension to traditional marketing in terms of a wider customer reach. It also enables the introduction of new online channels while keeping the record of their audience to enable storage, tracking, and monitoring via channel analytics. Based on this information, businesses can make better decisions. Digital marketing has been treated by businesses as a necessity for them to stay alive and survive, particularly during the COVID-19 pandemic.

The demand during the pandemic can be classified into two groups – essential and non-essential. The essential industry of demand which supplied the necessary items, such as groceries, toiletries, pharmacies, and pet supplies had overwhelmed businesses with orders. Meanwhile, the non-essential industries faced losing their businesses due to a lack in demand for goods such as luxuries, appliances, automobiles, hospitality, travel, and tourism. All the changes brought on by the COVID-19 pandemic may or may not stay. But the importance of all these occurrences is the preparation for any possibility of economic shock, and for the online sellers and buyers to consider the best option to increase and improve their digital touchpoints for online consumers rather than the physical touchpoints.

Digital marketing is essential for attracting new customers, creating more business transactions, and strengthening customer loyalty through constant brand recalls. It covers the demands and supply order within the country as well as throughout the world. This can help to increase global supply and demand interactions, hence increases exports and imports across countries. In this regard, it is evident that digital platforms help to transform businesses, and on a larger scale, the whole country's economy, and the world's economy.

3.6.1. Products and Services in Digital Economy

There are three types of demand and supply conditions on the digital platform. First of these is the supply and demand for digital products, followed by the supply and demand for tangible products, and the last type is the supply and demand for intangible products as summarized in Table 1.

3.6.1.1. Supply and Demand Features for Digital Products. The supply for digital products, such as software, subscribed online newspapers, and subscribed digital notes and materials is unlimited since the production of digital products can be duplicated. There are no constraints on the supply for the digital products, and they can reach customers with unlimited demands in the market. There are, however, barriers in obtaining digital products on many digital platforms. The only effect is that sellers or producers need to compete in terms of the innovation of the product itself, for example, the innovation of software with the latest technology or those with more additional features and packages.

Table 1. The Features of the Type of Demand and Supply Conditions in Digital Economy.

Type of Supply and Demand	Demand	Supply	Product	Pricing	Examples
Digital products	Unlimited	Unlimited	Unique	Moderate	Software, digital notes and materials
Tangible products	Unlimited	Limited	Homogenous	Low	Groceries, pharmacies
Intangible products	Limited	Limited	Unique	Low	Services such as proofreading

Source: Author's construction.

3.6.1.2. Supply and Demand for Tangible Products on Digital Platforms. Tangible products are physical products which customers can obtain in physical stores or shops. Supply for tangible products is limited since the final product is being sold on physical premises as well as on online platforms. The input for tangible products is also limited. It is vital to obtain the product since the tangible products cannot be duplicated. Since the tangible products are marketed on digital platforms, the advertisement of the product can reach the customers from anywhere that creates demands locally and globally. Thus, the demand for tangible products on digital platforms becomes unlimited as long as the product is still available. Moreover, the information of the products obtained symmetrically can lead to price competition. Meanwhile, the innovation of the uniqueness of the product can also improve the delivery system, and the after-sales service. Unlike others, the sellers cannot simply set their products at a high price because customers can compare prices from other sellers easily.

3.6.1.3. Supply and Demand for Intangible Products on Digital Platforms. Supply and demand for intangible products on digital platforms can be witnessed in platforms such as Agoda, Booking.com, and also some online classes. Intangible products are always related to services which involve three types of conditions. The first is real-time condition where sellers or producers give services, and customers receive the services at the same time. Examples are online classes, hotel and accommodation, and health treatment. The second condition is for sellers to supply services now, but for customers to consume later. Examples are proofreading services where the proofreader needs to do the editing work and to return the draft to the customer once it is finished.

The third one is to supply services later after receiving an item from the customer. Examples are delivery services, rating services, evaluation services, and publication services. Since intangible products are usually produced by order, the supply is limited. The demand is, however, unlimited since it is accessible anywhere.

4. SUPPLY SIDE RELATED TO DIGITAL TRANSFORMATION

Chunsheng Zhou, Professor of Finance, in his book, *Limitless Supply: The New Economy in the Digital Era*, stated that the limitless supply economy is one where products are supplied to more consumers, but at zero marginal cost (Zhou & Hu, 2022). These include WeChat, Tik Tok, and ZOOM. The growth of digital economy depends on the demand for digital services offered by digital companies, such as Meta, ZOOM, and Tik Tok which have become giants and market leaders in a relatively short period of time. Latecomers must thus, find niche markets, invent new products, create new business models, or produce higher quality products if they wish to survive and grow.

4.1. Digital Transformation and Production Efficiency

Digital transformation provides speed, convenience, and ease to the society. They make sure that products can be easily found, particularly when the smartphone is mapped and directed to the location of the item in the store. Digitalization adds value to the economy in terms of time saving, enhanced inventory checks, wide delivery options, and fast pick-up choices. In the process of digitalization, production efficiency is referred to as real-time updates. All stages in the production process can be tracked and updated through AI and the IoT. In Industry 4.0, the environment of manufacturing has led to a transparency system which enhances the flexibility of management and production (Bauer et al., 2015). A smart production system that increases the production rate, and accelerates the speed of production while minimizing mistakes is the main purpose of IR 4.0 (Schlaepfer et al., 2015).

4.2. Advertisement in the Digital Economy

According to the statistics of Cube Asia (2024), Shopee in Malaysia has the highest rate of visits, receiving over 50 million monthly web visits, followed by PG Mall (22.8 million), and Lazada (13.4 million). These top three platforms are ranked in terms of popularity of app downloads by millions of active social media engagements. Business popularity can be boosted by the social network which in turn, increases sales revenue. This happens because business advertising is usually published for free in the social network. This helps businesses to disclose their brands and products to the public effectively (Alturas & Almeida, 2015).

In business, social network marketing can be conducted through digital platforms for the sake of raising brand awareness among consumers, and for managing brand reputations. Social marketing involves ideas, skills as well as the analytical skill to understand the social impact of marketing plans used for improving the economy (Kelly & Lazer, 1973). A study conducted by Agnihotri et al. (2009) revealed that communication can be improved through sales technology because the latter is more flexible, and it offers more opportunities for businesses to share information with consumers. This can eventually develop customer relationships. To deepen these relationships between the consumers, and to increase collaborations, businesses could also use social media with other enterprises (Barker & Imam, 2008). This will allow businesses to reach more audiences based on the advertisements or through the recommendation of social media influencers (Kumaradeepan, 2020). In their study, Knoll and Matthes (2017) found that a good marketing strategy for businesses was to get someone who is well-known and has high social values to influence the consumers. Micro-influencers appeared to be more effective in encouraging others to engage with them as they were more personal (Chang et al., 2019).

4.3. Pricing and Profitability in Digital Economy

The marginal cost of limitless supply of products is zero; this means that producers can increase the supply without raising costs, especially if the product was data driven, or can be digitally duplicated. The price of products is determined by the type of business model. Digital products backed by technologies, such as Microsoft Windows or Tencent's WeChat, make it possible for their companies to expand by growing their customer base rather than by investing in fixed assets. Due to this attribute, companies with digital products, such as Alibaba, Tencent, ByteDance, Facebook, Google, and Amazon, focus on marketing as a measure to acquire as many users as possible, and to profit from the traffic created.

4.4. Delivery System in Digital Economy

The transaction between customers, sellers, and the payment gateway is interconnected with a fourth party, which is delivery. Its aim is to deliver the item to customers. Although the buying process on the digital platform is fast and easy, the delivery of the product is usually delayed. Customers are not able to consume the tangible or intangible products that they had purchased on the digital platforms, immediately. Hence, the utility maximization is delayed. The customer, however, can track the delivery and the progress of the order by using the digital platform supported by the IoT.

5. DEMAND SIDE RELATED TO THE DIGITAL TRANSFORMATION

Customer demands derived from online shopping are measured by the number of orders. The demand in the market via online shopping has different characteristics and implications. Easy payment with online transactions, for example, buy now pay later, is a form of payment that encourages more demands in the market.

5.1. Increasing Consumer's Choice of Product and Services

The overwhelming information and online businesses have allowed customers to have a variety of choices of products. The information offered by online marketing affects the psychological, personal, and social well-being of the consumers' choice. From a psychological well-being perspective, comprehensive information enables consumers to make informed decisions, reduce anxiety, and regret associated with purchases. Accessing online product information allows consumers to choose products that align with their self-image and values, enhancing their sense of identity and self-esteem which impacts the personal well-being of consumers. Businesses that maintain a strong presence on social media and online platforms can effectively engage with customers, fostering a sense of community and helping consumers feel connected to the brand. Additionally, reviews and discussions about products on online platforms create social connectivity and relationships, further enhancing the social well-being of consumers.

5.2. Increasing Consumer's Purchasing Power

If the price of one item is higher than the one offered by other sellers in the digital market, customers can easily move to the other sellers, without any cost. This makes market competition a perfect bid. To get the best offer, customers can easily survey the online market for the cheapest price for the same product. The sellers cannot simply increase the price since the price elasticity is high in a market where the information is symmetric. The high substitution price effect can increase consumers' purchasing power, and this is the factor that determines the online market price.

5.3. Increasing Consumer Awareness of the Product and Services

The information provided in online advertisements can increase consumers' awareness of the existence of the product and services. It is easy to market a new product or the innovative product by using digital marketing. To retain business in the market, the evaluation of the existing customers is important. Reviews from other customers reflecting their experiences on buying and consuming the products are one way. Good reviews can encourage more demands from customers on digital platforms while bad reviews will create caution for the new buyers.

5.4. Consumer Involvement in Increasing the Product Quality

Online businesses that provide space for customers to review can improve their business and product quality. For example, sellers can improve their product quality based on the information obtained from consumers' reviews, whether good or bad. Sellers need to address the issue quickly to ensure that the customer is still loyal to the business.

5.5. Reducing Asymmetric Information

It is easy for sellers to enter the market via digital platforms, but not vital for them to get the location and space in online business. Therefore, competitiveness in the digital market is high. An overwhelming amount of product information in the digital platforms can make customers compare products easily, such as the make, price, and delivery.

6. CHAPTER SUMMARY

Digital transformation provides many benefits to the Malaysian economy. It can create new markets, expand the economic space, increase market share, enhance transparency in transactions, improve accessibility across groups in the market as a seller or buyer, elevate competitiveness, develop workers' efficiency, and multiply production efficiency. Digital transformation is a paradigm shift that is useful for restructuring the economy, taking the industry from asymmetry to symmetric information on the market. It reduces the barrier for SMEs to enter the market and instead encourages more new SMEs to stimulate the economy.

Through digital platforms, normal people and people with disabilities can conduct businesses from homes, with less risk of physical mobility. These disabled persons can generate income from the digital platforms as an entrepreneur, or a content creator, or an influencer. In addition, digital transformation creates accessibility for employers to hire workers, and for employees to apply for jobs. Employees, including foreign staff, can still contribute to the organization with remote work facilities. Employers can also engage foreign employees who have the expertise at lesser costs. With the high accessibility of work made possible on digital platforms, more gig activities in the gig economy can be stimulated. The mobility constraints seen during the movement control order caused by the COVID-19 pandemic had witnessed the dynamics of digital transformation assisting many SMEs to survive and explore the new market.

REFERENCES

Agnihotri, R., Dingus, R., Hu, M. Y., & Krush, M. T. (2016). Social media: Influencing customer satisfaction in B2B sales. *Industrial Marketing Management*, *53*, 172–180.

Agnihotri, R., Rapp, A., & Trainor, K. (2009). Understanding the role of information communication in the buyer–seller exchange process: Antecedents and outcomes. *Journal of Business & Industrial Marketing*, *24*(7), 474–486.

Alturas, B., & Almeida, C. (2015). *Social networks as a platform for business marketing*. CBR European Marketing Conference 2015. Lisbon, Portugal.

Anderl, R. (2015). Industrie 4.0 – Technological approaches, use cases, and implementation. *at-Automatisierungstechnik*, *63*(10), 753–765.

Aral, S., & Weill, P. (2007). IT assets, organizational capabilities, and firm performance: How resource allocations and organizational differences explain performance variation. *Organization Science*, *18*(5), 763–780.

Bahri, E. N. A., & Min, W. (2023). Job creation vs job destruction following Industrial Revolution 4.0. In M. N. Almunawar, P. O. de Pablos & M. Anshari (Eds.) *Digital transformation for business and society: Contemporary issues and applications in Asia* (pp. 1–21). Routledge.

Barker, R., & Imam, S. (2008). Analysts' perceptions of 'earnings quality'. *Accounting and Business Research*, *38*(4), 313–329.

Bauer, W., Hämmerle, M., Schlund, S., & Vocke, C. (2015). Transforming to a hyper-connected society and economy – Towards an "Industry 4.0". *Procedia Manufacturing*, *3*, 417–424.

Berman, S. J. (2012). Digital transformation: Opportunities to create new business models. *Strategy & Leadership*, *40*(2), 16–24.

Berriman, R., & Hawksworth, J. (2017). *Will Robots Steal our Jobs? The Potential Impact of Automation on the UK and other Major Economies.* PwC UK Economic Outlook.

Bessen, J. (2015). Toil and technology: Innovative technology is displacing workers to new jobs rather than replacing them entirely. *Finance & Development*, *52*(001), 16.

Bilal, M., Zhang, Y., Cai, S., Akram, U., & Halibas, A. (2024). Artificial intelligence is the magic wand making customer-centric a reality! An investigation into the relationship between consumer purchase intention and consumer engagement through affective attachment. *Journal of Retailing and Consumer Services*, *77*, 103674.

Braojos-Gomez, J., Benitez-Amado, J., & Llorens-Montes, F. J. (2015). How do small firms learn to develop a social media competence? *International Journal of Information Management*, *35*(4), 443–458.

Bughin, J., Chui, M., & Manyika, J. (2012). Capturing business value with social technologies. *McKinsey Quarterly*, *4*(1), 72–80.

Chang, Y., Li, Y., Yan, J., & Kumar, V. (2019). Getting more likes: the impact of narrative person and brand image on customer-brand interactions. *Journal of the Academy of Marketing Science*, *47*(6), 1027–1045.

Chang, V., Walters, R.J., & Wills, G. (2013). The development that leads to the Cloud Computing Business Framework. *International Journal of Information Management*, *33*(3), 524–538.

Costa, R., Dias, A., Pereira, L., Santos, J., & Capelo, A. (2019). The impact of artificial intelligence on commercial management. *Problems and Perspectives in Management*, *17*(4), 441–452.

Costa, E., Soares, A.L., & Sousa, J.P.D. (2020). Industrial business associations improving the internationalisation of SMEs with digital platforms: A design science research approach. *International Journal of Information Management*, *53*, 102070.

Cova, B., Pace, S., & Park, D. J. (2007). Global brand communities across borders: The Warhammer case. *International Marketing Review*, *24*(3), 313–329.

Cube Asia. (2024, November 25). Shopee's GMV Increased 29.1% from 2023 to 2024: Its Past Performance Shows the Future Looks Bright, by Affifa. *Cube Asia*. https://cube.asia/shopee-gmv-growth-2023-2024-shows-bright-future/

David, F. R., & David, F. R. (2017). *Strategic management: Concepts and cases: A competitive advantage approach*. Pearson.

Durkin, M., McGowan, P., & McKeown, N. (2013). Exploring social media adoption in small to medium-sized enterprises in Ireland. *Journal of Small Business and Enterprise Development*, *20*(4), 716–734.

Fruhling, A. L., & Digman, L. A. (2000). The impact of electronic commerce on business-level strategies. *Journal of Electronic Commerce Research*, *1*(1), 13.

George, A., & Sunny, P. (2021). Developing a research model for mobile wallet adoption and usage. *IIM Kozhikode Society & Management Review*, *10*(1), 82–98.

He, X. J. (2014). Business intelligence and big data analytics: An overview. *Communications of the IIMA*, *14*(3), 1.

Hoffman, A.L., Proferes, N., & Zimmer, M. (2018). "Making the world more open and connected": Mark Zuckerberg and the discursive construction of Facebook and its users. *New Media and Society*, *20*(1), 199–218.

Ismail, I. (2019, October 14). 2020 Budget: A boost for Malaysia's tech industry. *New Straits Times*. https://www.nst.com.my/lifestyle/bots/2019/10/529831/2020-budget-boost-malaysias-tech-industry

Kaplan, A., & Haenlein, M. (2019). Siri, Siri, in My Hand: Who's the Fairest in the Land? On the Interpretations, Illustrations, and Implications of Artificial Intelligence. *Business Horizons*, *62*, 15–25.

Kelly, E. J., & Lazer, W. (1973). *Managerial marketing*. Irwin.

Knoll, J., & Matthes, J. (2017). The effectiveness of celebrity endorsements: A meta-analysis. *Journal of the Academy of Marketing Science*, *45*, 55–75.

Kumaradeepan, V. (2020). Social Media Advertising As Strategy On Consumer Buying Behaviour: Conceptual paper. *Journal of Management*, *15*(2), 30–37.

Mangold, W. G., & Faulds, D. J. (2009). Social media: The new hybrid element of the promotion mix. *Business Horizons*, *52*(4), 357–365.

Manyika, J., Chui, M., Bughin, J., Dobbs, R., Bisson, P., & Marrs, A. (2013, May). *Disruptive technologies: Advances that will transform life, business, and the global economy*. McKinsey Global Institute.

McCann, M., & Barlow, A. (2015). Use and measurement of social media for SMEs. *Journal of Small Business and Enterprise Development*, 22(2), 273–287.

McKinsey. (2013). *How companies are benefiting from Web 2.0* | https://www.mckinsey.com/capabilities/mckinsey-digital/our-insights/how-companies-are-benefiting-from-web-20-mckinsey-global-survey-results

Michaelidou, N., Siamagka, N. T., & Christodoulides, G. (2011). Usage, barriers and measurement of social media marketing: An exploratory investigation of small and medium B2B brands. *Industrial Marketing Management*, *40*(7), 1153–1159.

McCulloch, J.R. (1821). The opinions of Messrs. say, Sismondi, and Malthus on the effects of machinery and accumulation, stated and examined. *Edinburgh Review*, *35*, 102–123.

Muhammad, M. Z., Char, A. K., bin Yasoa, M. R., & Hassan, Z. (2010). Small and medium enterprises (SMEs) competing in the global business environment: A case of Malaysia. *International Business Research*, *3*(1), 66.

Perna, M.C. (2019, December 27). Gen Z Is Already Changing The World – Just Ask Time's 2019 Person Of The Year. *Forbes*. https://www.forbes.com/sites/markcperna/2019/12/27/gen-z-is-already-changing-the-world-just-ask-times-2019-person-of-the-year/

Petrosyan, A. (2024, Nov 5). Worldwide digital population 2024. *Statista*. https://www.statista.com/statistics/617136/digital-population-worldwide/#:~:text=Worldwide%20digital%20population%202024&text=As%20of%20October%202024%2C%20there,population%2C%20were%20social%20media%20users.

Porter, M. E. (2001). Strategy and the internet. *Harvard Business Review*, *79*(2), 62–78.

Purcell, J. (2014). Disengaging from engagement. *Human Resource Management Journal*, *24*(3), 241–254.

Schlaepfer, R. C., Koch, M., & Merkofer, P. (2015). *Deloitte, Industry 4.0: Challenges and solutions for the digital transformation, and use of exponential technologies*. Retrieved October 16, 2017, from https://

www2.deloitte.com/content/dam/Deloitte/ch/Documents/manufacturing/ch-enmanufacturing-industry-4-0-24102014.pdf

Schwab, K. (2017). *The fourth industrial revolution.* Currency.

Siddiqui, S., & Singh, T. (2016). Social media its impact with positive and negative aspects. *International Journal of Computer Applications Technology and Research*, *5*(2), 71–75.

Siddharta, A. (2024, Jun 7). Social media in Malaysia – statistics & facts. *Statista.* https://www.statista.com/topics/10858/social-media-in-malaysia/#topicOverview

Stephen, A. T., & Galak, J. (2012). The effects of traditional and social earned media on sales: A study of a microlending marketplace. *Journal of Marketing Research*, *49*(5), 624–639.

Susskind, R., & Susskind, D. (2016, Oct 11). Technology will replace many doctors, lawyers, and other professionals. *Harvard Business Review.* https://hbr.org/2016/10/robots-will-replace-doctors-lawyers-and-other-professionals

Trusov, M., Bucklin, R. E., & Pauwels, K. (2009). Effects of word-of-mouth versus traditional marketing: Findings from an internet social networking site. *Journal of Marketing*, *73*(5), 90–102.

Tsao, W. C., & Chang, H. R. (2010). Exploring the impact of personality traits on online shopping behavior. *African Journal of Business Management*, *4*(9), 1800–1812.

UNCTAD. (2022). *World Investment Report 2022: International Tax Reforms and Sustainable Investment.* United Nations publication. Sales No. E.21.II.D.20. New York and Geneva.

Wang, D., & Shao, X. (2024). Research on the impact of digital transformation on the production efficiency of manufacturing enterprises: Institution-based analysis of the threshold effect. *International Review of Economics & Finance*, *91*, 883–897.

Woodward, M. (2024, Jun 23). Social Media User Statistics: How Many People Use Social Media? *Search Logistics.* https://www.searchlogistics.com/learn/statistics/social-media-user-statistics/

Zhang, Z., Liu, S., & Tang, M. (2014). Industry 4.0: Challenges and opportunities for Chinese manufacturing industry. *Tehnicki Vjesnik-Technical Gazette*, *21*(6), III+.

Zhou, C., & Hu, X. (2022). *Limitless supply: New economy in the digital era.* World Scientific Publisher.

3

IMPACT OF DIGITAL TRANSFORMATION ON BUSINESS FUNCTIONAL AREAS OF SMEs

ABSTRACT

Rapid technological advancement has transformed businesses especially the small and medium enterprises (SMEs) in Malaysia. This has led to digital transformation in a larger scale during the COVID-19 pandemic since there were restrictions in terms of mobility, contributing to the surge of online shopping. While many people have adopted technology during that period, some others are still struggling to adopt to the new norm. This chapter investigates the impact of digital transformation across operations, marketing, customer service, accounting, and finance areas. Not a single department can work in silo, hence it is vital to observe the digital transformation in the main business areas to create a competitive advantage besides being resilience to both internal and external factors that influence the business operation. This can provide insights to the business on the overall value creation in converting inputs to output. The technological advancement takes place at a fast rate; thus, the business will need to be agile in adapting to the changes. This chapter will explore the nature of adoption and ways to go about it in the different business areas to avoid haphazard technology adoption which can have an adverse impact on the business. The large organizations like multinational corporations are not an exception to face pressure in coping with the fast-paced technology evolvement, alongside with the SMEs. However, this should not hinder the SMEs from engaging in digital transformation.

Keywords: Malaysia; SMEs; digital transformation; digitalization; functional areas

1. INTRODUCTION

As discussed in earlier chapters, the rapid advancement of technology has changed the business landscape worldwide, especially during the COVID-19 pandemic, two and a half years ago. The movement control order that was imposed by the Malaysian government in the country had affected the businesses run by SMEs. During the pandemic, many did not survive due to the scarcity of resources, and their lack of resilience. Although digitalization drives competitiveness, Tong and Gong (2020) noted that it was the bleak outlook of economy that had driven businesses to digital adoption as a measure to sustain themselves. Previously, they thrived on the old approach of brick and mortar, but automation and higher levels of digital technology had spurred business growth. The digital evolution caused business operators to embrace technology, particularly during the COVID-19 period of uncertainty. One such initiative spurred by the government to boost the economy was Malaysia Digital. It was developed to encourage local companies to become a part of the 'global digital revolution' and 'digital economy'. To further enhance the digital ecosystem, it was therefore necessary for all parties to play their roles, and the Malaysia Digital Economy Corporation emphasized that all entrepreneurs, SMEs, and corporations are essential players.

The Malaysian government supports the adoption of digital technology and platforms which were created to help SMEs to conduct their businesses and also to revitalize the country's economy. While larger corporations take to the change more readily, SMEs tend to take lesser risks (Deniz, 2021). Anyhow, with digital evolution, they have to adapt if they wish to sustain their businesses in the long run. Rapid technological advancement leads to stiff business competition; hence SMEs need to leverage on the technology so as to enhance productivity and better customer services.

Technological evolvement can influence the transition and transformation of businesses, and their components include big data, machine learning, internet of things (IOT), virtual reality (VR), artificial intelligence (AI), mixed reality (MR), cloud computing, and metaverse. Put together, these components are vital for SMEs because this technological evolution can improve business processes (Jurgielewicz, 2019; Morakanyane et al., 2017), enhance business automation (Joao Carlos et al., 2018; Morakanyane et al., 2017), facilitate customer engagement and experience (Joao Carlos et al., 2018; Morakanyane et al., 2017), and also accelerate business operations and the supply chain (Jurgielewicz, 2019).

The fast-changing environment of businesses is forcing many companies to transform because the digital gap will widen if they fail to do so. Past research on the entrepreneurship ecosystem had indicated that both the government and the industry are the catalysts of digital transformation (OECD, 2019). Thus, the government has to ensure that there are adequate policy-making strategies and regulatory plans for the benefit of encouraging the growth of SMEs in the country.

2. DIGITAL TRANSFORMATION IN BUSINESS FUNCTIONAL AREAS

Digital transformation is evident in many sectors, such as operations, marketing, customer services, accounting, and finance. The section below will focus on how the digital transformation had impacted the various functional areas of business.

2.1. Digital Transformation in Operations

The transition mode of moving from 'labour intensive to automation' (Khin & Hung, 2022) was driven by the digital transformation that was impacting the manufacturing industry. It changed the way products were manufactured, and how decision-making was processed (Cotteleer & Sniderman, 2017). It converted conventional manufacturing to smart manufacturing, where production systems were designed to enable companies to make their own decisions (Marr, 2016). With the prevalence of AI, businesses are now able to capitalize on modern robotics that increase productivity and reduce human reliance on workforce (Khin & Kee, 2022).

In line with Industry Revolution 4.0, the Malaysian government also launched the National Policy, Industry 4WRD. It was meant to encourage more SMEs to become involved in the digitalization process due to low adoption rates (Khin & Kee, 2022). Business growth, after the introduction of the technology, had been slow and the country's productivity and efficiency were dependent on their level of adoption rate (Horváth & Szabó, 2019). The government had wanted to raise more technology awareness among the

SMEs thus, it began highlighting the benefits of digital transformation and its perceived benefits on business growth to the industry. The pull factors of smart products and smart production processes were especially useful because they paved the way for businesses to improve their manufacturing processes, especially in smart factories. For instance, automation of the manufacturing process would accelerate product customization and fulfil various customer needs. Mass production of certain products would be made easier, and sales scales could be achieved, thereby enabling businesses to maintain sustainability.

For businesses to transform, they had to make decisions, and these decisions of operating their businesses can affect their business costs and productivity. Those decisions, however, can be influenced by a number of factors, such as market demands (Ratnasingam et al., 2020), and competitive pressures (Horváth & Szabó, 2019). Inevitably, companies need to decide whether they should be transforming digitally in order to stay competitive. Their businesses would, of course, lose out to their competitors who had actively adopted the new technology. Nevertheless, the intensity of the competitive pressure faced by companies may vary among industries (Khin & Kee, 2022). In this regard, companies' readiness in adopting certain operational systems may have to be dependent on the resources available to them as well as the accessibility of infrastructure.

Following the lean manufacturing era, Industry 4.0 and its technology are now geared towards speeding up the performance of businesses and the enhancement of products/services provided. This technology is expected to increase the rate of automation, and to enhance customer value creation (Buer et al., 2021). Improvement is more evident in the manufacturing activities (Buer et al., 2021) which tend to use various components such as digital sensors, the IoT, artificial intelligence of things, big data analytics, and also blockchain technology (Brynjolfsson & McAfee, 2014; Jing, 2023; Kagermann et al., 2013) to speed up their manufacturing process. While the digitalization process is unavoidable it can be hindered by factors such as costs, security, novelty of technology, and its barriers followed by the subsequent impact it could cause to businesses such as the need to develop new business models.

The transformation for SMEs is riskier due to their limited access to technological resources (Jing, 2023). As a matter of fact, digitalization adoption is low among SMEs, compared to larger corporations. This implies that the business sector has a higher need for digital tools that can help them to operate their businesses. Jing (2023) stated that collaborative models such as 'Platform + Independent Software Vendor (ISV)' can be used by SMEs to enhance their penetration level into digitalization. Nonetheless, this model needs to cater to the dynamic nature of the business operations since efficiency could be affected by the use of automation, and the streamlining of activities.

In the context of SMEs, supply chain management is vital for business sustainability because it involves various activities which range from obtaining raw materials until the product is sold to the customer (Goyat et al., 2019; Menon & Shah, 2019). The blockchain technology is vital for transforming the supply chain management process in SMEs because it reduces costs and increases product quality and operational speed (Kshetri, 2018). The blockchain technology facilitates better decision-making, increases product traceability, provides product deletion, and offers price tracking and transparency. Therefore, blockchain reduces risks involved in the supply chain (Dutta et al., 2020; Kshetri, 2018).

Another technology that improves the supply chain operations of an organization is Enterprise Resource Planning (ERP) (Banerjee, 2018). It has the ability to improve coordination between the channel members such as the suppliers, distributors, and the retailers. The coordination will help SMEs to distribute their products to customers in a timely manner which in turn, affects customers' overall satisfaction. The ERP system helps inventory management by reducing excess time tracking. Real-time tracking enables SMEs to reduce warehousing costs while also improving production schedules. The advancement of the Just-in-Time inventory system is driven by production agility, which enhances inventory turnover and reduces stockouts, minimizes waste, and boosts operational efficiency by minimizing delays. The seamless communication and data-driven process allow the organizations to leverage big data, allowing SMEs to predict inventory precisely and make informed decisions (Feroz et al., 2021; Garamendi-Colos et al., 2020; Warner & Wäger, 2019). It also minimizes disruptions besides enhancing responsiveness in the supply chain.

Digitization is a process that automates and streamlines operational processes; it is also a key player in the supply chain management and the inventory control system of SMEs. This implies that the adoption of technology is necessary to improve the internal operations of SMEs.

2.2. Digital Transformation in Marketing

It is vital for SMEs to understand the 'new digital technologies and processes' (Kee et al., 2023) since digital transformation provides businesses with a better market opportunity. When applied, digital transformation affects the product design, the manufacturing process, the way a product/service is delivered to the customer, and it offers data-driven services (Sundblad, 2018). Therefore, businesses have no choice but to adopt/adapt the new technology into their business operations (Kee et al., 2023).

The core competencies of the business may change depending on how the new technology is embraced. As an illustration, the advent of digital transformation has led to the development of smart products which likewise also meet the needs and wants of customers. The demand for such products will in turn increase because of the convenience given to customers and the satisfaction they achieved after getting an enhanced overall experience of using such products (Horváth & Szabó, 2019). This could inevitably, gain businesses customer loyalty. In this regard, it is timely for business operators to flow with the customer-oriented approach so as to maintain customer loyalty. Nonetheless, digital transformation may likewise, pose some challenges to SMEs in the marketing aspect.

For example, digitalization in the marketing aspect can increase the business' potential to expand, thus could adversely affect the sustainability of the business in the long run, given the limited resources to expand eventually. Many SMEs today are still operating their businesses in the traditional brick and mortar method even though digital transformation has been rapid. Digitalization accelerated during the COVID-19 pandemic when most businesses had no choice but to resort to online sales and transactions due to restricted mobility. There were no physical interactions with customers and payments had to be conducted online. Consequently, businesses which were performing mainly through digitalization saw a change in their revenue. For example, DeliverEat.my which operates in Kuala Lumpur and Penang, reported an increase of 300% sales for both regions, during the COVID-19 pandemic. A similar trend was also observed in food transactions by Foodpanda, Grabfood, and Shopeefood (Bernama, 2020, March 18).

Digitalization played a crucial role during the crisis. It was mentioned by the Azalea and Nehru (2024) that digitalization became more rapid due to the force to vendors in adopting it for their business operations. If left to their own initiatives to conduct their businesses online, digitalization would have suffered because most vendors were not technology savvy, hence they would be reluctant to be part of digitalization. To encourage more digital transformation among the SMEs, the Small and Medium Enterprises Association Malaysia (SAMENTA) is thus strongly urging these SMEs to adopt AI and digitalization tools so as to stay competitive (Santani, 2024).

In the business context, marketing is all about creating values to fulfil customer needs. However, this occurs at different stages/processes of the business as companies strive to be more competitive, and to provide the best to their customers. In this regard, the marketing team needs to assess the costs and benefits in order to determine the worthiness of implementing these marketing strategies. Digitization in marketing could increase visibility, define target audience as well as build and strengthen customer relationship. It also helps an organization during the post purchase/after-sale stage since it is vital to establish relationship marketing instead of transactional marketing. Even though the boom of e-commerce was witnessed during COVID-19, about 34% of SMEs had been adversely affected by it in Malaysia. Many SMEs could not survive due to financial issues, and as a result, they depend on government support during the crisis. These SMEs experienced a drop in sales, and limited market accessibility because many were physical in nature (Vaghefi & Jo-yee, 2021). Due to their lack of resources, knowledge, and skills, these SMEs suffered and were unable to sustain their former physical glory.

One of the older payment platforms of online transactions, PayPal (2022), had reported that only 39% of Malaysian SMEs' advertising and marketing had been digitized. This shows that online presence of a product/service offered by Malaysian businesses is still low even though it is essential to the current business world. The focus of many businesses today appears to centre on search engine optimization, email marketing, content marketing, lead enrichment, affiliate marketing, and social media engagement. These are used at various stages to create awareness of the product/service so that there is customer consideration and finally, conversion.

The success of marketing tactics and strategies is closely linked to the conversion rate, which includes generating leads, prompting calls to action, and driving purchasing behaviour. Therefore, the initial stages of creating awareness and fostering consideration are crucial for guiding customers further along the sales funnel. Ultimately, return on investment reflects the effectiveness of these conversions. Businesses are trying to maintain their existing customer base because it is extremely costly to acquire a new customer base. By doing so, SMEs need to be aware of the prevalent digital tools, and how they can be integrated so as to delight the customers. Notably, merely satisfying customers is no longer sufficient in the competitive business environment.

Among the ways that SMEs attempt to touch base, and to stay connected with their current and potential customers are to optimize their search engines, create websites, and utilize social media platforms. These strategies are cost effective and faster to reach the audience, compared to traditional means. They also allow SMEs to better utilize their resources as well as to engage the targeted audience besides providing customers with personalized messages. Given the reduced attention span of customers, the message(s) or content(s) need to be short and precise so that the customers can grasp and act accordingly. This implies that the relevance of the message plays a vital role in determining the way customers act and react.

On the other hand, content marketing is a 'tool designed to establish long-term and intensive emotion-based relationships with a brand' (Ziółkowska, 2021, p. 8). In the case of SMEs, the relevant approach in the form of website, short video, or picture, is important to use if businesses wish to communicate with their customers. Frequent communication could accelerate brand recognition and brand association, especially when the scene is crowded. The boom of social influencers had resulted in various benefits to SMEs and thus, excessive messages or contents are not welcomed because they can dilute the presence of small businesses faster than ever. This means that SMEs should maintain public relations through their online presence although they would need to be innovative and resourceful in order to stay relevant. Clearly, digital marketing contents can be powerful if practised appropriately, given the acceleration of digital transformation in Malaysian SMEs.

There are about 1.1 million MSMEs expected to adopt e-commerce by 2025 (PayPal, 2022). These digitally transformed businesses have been actively utilizing social media platform like Facebook, Instagram, Twitter, TikTok, LinkedIn, YouTube, WhatsApp, Signal, Telegram, and TikTok to generate businesses. The internet and smartphone penetration has also contributed to the high usage of social media among Malaysians. This gives SMEs vast opportunities to tap into the targeted market and to advertise their products/services. Digital advertisement spending in Malaysia accounted for $109 billion in 2023. The rise of e-commerce and digital transformation presents significant opportunities for MSMEs in Malaysia, it is timely for them to adopt these changes and expand their reach beyond national borders. By diversifying their distribution channels based on their target markets, they can enable customers to purchase what they want, when they want, and how they prefer. Effectively serving the right customers in the right way can lead to exponential business growth, highlighting a shift from transactional marketing to relationship-focussed marketing. The growth of online user activities and digital banner advertisement indicates the reliance of social media usage among the consumers in Malaysia (Meltwater, 2024).

SMEs can utilize Facebook advertisement, short videos on TikTok, and pictures on Instagram to reach their customers virtually and easily. Businesses can also choose to send personalized messages via social media to customers based on the usage algorithm in order to create brand exposure and to increase customer engagement. Malaysian consumers are now using social media platforms far beyond networking; social media platforms are recently being used for other purposes, such as making reservations/bookings, rescheduling, ticket purchasing, cancellations, and also to provide customer feedback. The usage of social media in the SMEs cannot be underestimated as it affects the market presence and brand equity (Alias et al., 2022; Razak et al., 2023).

Today hashtags are making waves on social media; they guide people to the contents that they are interested. Trending hashtags can increase customer lead and engagement as it creates noise about brands or issues. Businesses need to be aware of the latest trends and controversial issues. The saying 'bad marketing is good marketing' indicates that engaging in some sort of marketing is better than having no marketing at all. The buzz it creates will increase customer awareness and more brand exposure.

The digital economy has boosted digital transformation in Malaysia through developments like digital payment, e-wallet, online banking, QR payments, and digital currency payment. The adoption of digital payment clearly offers more benefits to businesses. However, sometimes there are other factors hindering its usage among Malaysian SMEs, such as high transaction fees and difficulties in integrating online sales platform (PayPal, 2022). Since customers today are technology savvy, it is advisable for SMEs to integrate their digital payment platforms, especially with their presence growing online. In this case, big data in digital technology can help businesses to identify the various patterns and correlations of purchases, and this can really enable companies to grow faster and to make wiser decisions. Real-time data captured can be used for targeting and marketing communication purposes since they offer information on what would be the ideal target market, and what kind of messages should be spread via the appropriate channels. Businesses can conduct their market intelligence, and then target new customers accordingly as information about the customers' preferences is released for businesses to retain customers, and to find new ones.

2.3. Digital Transformation in Customer Service

Today's business landscape has been changed by various disruptive technologies which include AI, VR, augmented reality (AR), MR, extended reality (XR), big data, and cloud computing. Among them, XR is an umbrella term used to refer to VR, AR, and MR collectively as a spatially immersive ecosystem that enables immersive learning (Moro et al., 2020, p. 370). With Technology 4.0, it would appear that there is also Marketing 4.0 which is there to propel businesses to be more innovative when catering to customers as well as to improve customer interactions (Dimitrova et al., 2024).

The combination of AR, VR, and MR paves the way for endless marketing possibilities for SMEs such as product innovation, business models, and service offerings (Pessot et al., 2023). It was observed by Tsang et al. (2022) that augmented-reality interactive technology can help businesses to improve their retail experiences since virtual platforms enable customers to virtually try on apparels based on their appearance. This seamless experience enhances brand loyalty and customer relationship. One illustration is the use of Go Pro's impressions of 360° video which had helped to improve user experiences (Burton & Schlieman, 2021).

Meanwhile, AI can be used to diversify marketing channels, building from single channels to multiple channels until the incorporation of omnichannels (Ziółkowska, 2021). The integration of both the physical and online channels (omni-channel) offers customers a broad and seamless experience. This practice is mostly applied by big corporations compared to SMEs in which the latter are constantly restricted by limited resources. Nevertheless, their online presence can be boosted with the use of simple tools like Google Analytics, and Google Ads which can provide insights on traffic directed to the websites or the social media sites of SMEs. There is various software that can be used to create and organize contents, manage social media, provide personalized message, manage customer relationship, and optimize conversions.

Freelance technological experts are also easily available should they be required to assist SMEs in utilizing these tools. Social media tools provide opportunities for the business to maintain online presence besides creating content relevant to the target audience across different channels. The tools can assist SMEs to create their marketing campaigns, boost sales, manage customer experience, increase customer retention, enhance customer satisfaction, and customer loyalty. The SMEs can leverage on these tools for decision-making and foster business growth with limited resources.

Customer relationship management (CRM) has evolved over the years due to digitalization. Today, SMEs are using both the CRM and ERP software to manage customer interactions by providing them with personalized services. Hassan et al. (2019) examined the viewpoints of Muslim SME owners in Malaysia with regard to the advantages offered by social customer relationship management (s-CRM). They found that perceived value drove the adoption of customer information management. This suggests that by leveraging on technology, SMEs have the comparative advantage of speed and convenience when approaching customers, unlike conventional approaches which consumed more time and efforts. SMEs were thus propelled to digitalize their CRM due to the limited access to customers and the restricted speed in disseminating information. The scope of CRM ranges from sales tracking, automated marketing, customer behaviour/pattern analysis to sales and targeted marketing. Evidence showed that the efficient management of customers would enhance customer communication, customer retention, and also data management.

The emergence of virtual agents is evident in many sectors as can be seen in the use of chatbots and virtual assistants by companies providing real-time assistance to customer queries through the help of machine learning. This practice provides personalized service at a faster rate; it enriches customer service, reduces waiting time, and it minimizes the dependency on 'real agent' because it can resolve many issues simultaneously. Machine learning enables the companies concerned to better understand the users based on the interactions, hence it is able to propose a suitable solution. In the event that the virtual agent is unable to provide a solution to complex issue(s), the human agent would then take over the communication by offering a personalized service. The take-over takes time and thus, the customer would still need to deal with the virtual agent initially, causing customer dissatisfaction in the service delivery.

The use of chatbots and virtual assistants is, however, limited because of the SMEs' settings which incur high costs for the processing power (Borah et al., 2022; Sharma et al., 2022). While integration is important, it is also complex. For instance, integrating AI into a business' operating system is both difficult and costly; that serves as the reason for its low adoption rate. Sharma et al. (2022), however, noted that there is a way to support SMEs which is through cloud computing. It is a good strategy that can assist SMEs that are faced with financial constraints. Besides costs and complexity, the integration of AI into business also involves other concerns associated with the use of chatbots and virtual assistants, such as trust and privacy issues. Data are collected and stored, but it is not clear how these data were being treated in terms of confidentiality, and the measures which are used to keep them safe.

Another aspect of digitalization for SMEs concerns the integration of emotional intelligence (EI) with AI as a step towards making the virtual assistants more humanlike or close-to-reality. The introduction of EI can impact on how these virtual assistants communicate with the customers, thus with insights, they would be better equipped to handle complicated and complex cases. Good communication would result in high customer engagement and retention as well as increased company revenue (Borah et al., 2022). Although the automation of customer service can improve efficiency and customer satisfaction, it appears to be indirectly reducing the reliance on human capital.

2.4. Digital Transformation in Accounting and Finance

For businesses to adopt new technologies, awareness and the availability of financial resources are necessary (Horváth & Szabó, 2019; Khin & Kee, 2022; Silva et al., 2020). Companies with stronger financial capabilities tend to utilize their own funds rather than rely on external fundings, when engaging in digital transformation (Horváth & Szabó, 2019). Effective accounting and financial management are essential to streamline and automate the process. Better cash flow management provides investment opportunities besides mitigating the risks involved. The real-time data and reporting capabilities help the organization to assess the business decisions and navigate the fluctuations in the market. The adaptability of the business to the changing environment would help SMEs to stay resilient (Ulas, 2019).

Nurzafirah et al. (2022) investigated the impact of digitalization on accounting practices among SMEs in Malaysia. They found that the administration data processing method needs to be digitalized. Meanwhile, Hasbolah et al. (2021) revealed that the sustainability of rural MSMEs was influenced by digital accounting entrepreneurship. It also appears that the digitization of accounts can affect SMEs' productivity, performance, competitiveness, and profitability (Pan & Lee, 2020; Przychocka & Sikorski, 2024). It was further reported that financial reports and accounting information had to be streamlined in order to increase accuracy. This is crucial for making wise decisions (Winarsih & Buyong, 2020) pertaining to resource allocation, risk management, investment decision, and securing fundings besides regulatory compliance. Clearly, automation in accounting and finance is paramount for improving efficiency, financial transparency, and profitability. Any error found in the financial and accounting data could lead to adverse effects on SMEs, such as a loss of trust and brand reputation.

The adequate tools used in advance reporting could help business owners to make wise and right decision(s), particularly when being viewed from the aspect of cash flow as well as profit and loss statements. Furthermore, digitization capitalizes on cloud computing. In this case, the use of Microsoft Excel and Access can ease the financial recordings and transactions of SMEs (Winarsih & Buyong, 2020). As a result, the automation ability afforded by technology also enables SMEs to make better evaluations of their businesses and within a shorter time period. This leads to better decision-making for the owners. This shows that digitalization makes it easier for businesses to conduct supervision, and to monitor both their accounting and financial data.

Apart from the above stated components, SMEs also need to conduct training on cloud accounting, digital invoices, and the use of financial and accounting tools for their employees so as to avoid underutilizing the new technology. Relevant government agencies also need to provide digital literacy training to SMEs in order to increase the adoption rate. Apart from that, SMEs must learn to be more aware of the degree of complexity involved in digital transformation. For example, digital accounting can save time too and it can analyse large amounts of data for prompt decisions. The cloud-based accounting system today is driving innovation; its impact is beyond operational effectiveness because it can save cost, improve transparency, and create convenience for users. SMEs hence, must be wise in choosing the right tools or software for their own business operations by taking into account the scale of their businesses, their current accounting practices, and the processes involved.

One aspect of digitalization is the use of electronic invoicing and payment methods, both of which offer several benefits such as easing information sharing, mitigating risks, providing real-time reporting, detecting purchase orders and delayed payments, and generating invoices as well as conveying a seamless integration of tools needed. Not so long ago, the Malaysian government had imposed e-invoicing as a ruling for businesses, such as SMEs that earn more than MYR150,000 annually. This ruling had compelled SMEs to convert to e-invoicing which allows them to track their financial standing in real time. The ability to access a detailed analysis generated by technology can also help SMEs to make better and wiser decisions based on both current and forecasted financial statement of the organization.

Digital invoicing and digital payments also benefit customers in various ways. For instance, they can experience transparent services, have alternative virtual payment channels, and have diverse options for payments. Pleasure customer experience can enhance customers' overall satisfaction and affect their intention to retain or even to recommend the product or service to others. Digitization also offers SMEs a better platform in terms of security and authentication since it is regulated by the government. While fraud cases can be minimized in digitalization, the risk of cybersecurity is still prevalent. This issue is more relevant to SMEs when they attempt to integrate their old business model with the new ones. If there is incompatibility, their business operations may be affected. Thus, SMEs need to have proper planning. The automation process and the improvement of their internal communication system reflect the value of digitization which has been emphasized by Przychocka and Sikorski (2024) as important in the growth of Industry 4.0. SMEs need it to manage their businesses effectively and to stay relevant and sustainable.

Fig. 1 illustrates the type of digital transformation taking place in the various business sectors among SMEs in Malaysia. Within operations, the

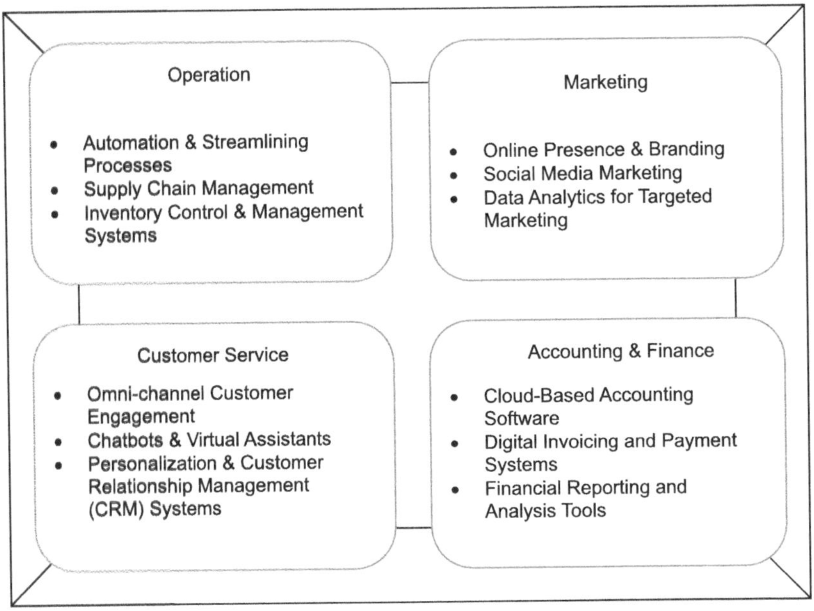

Fig. 1. The Digital Transformation of Business Areas Among SMEs in Malaysia.

automation process can increase speed, minimize errors, and reduce costs. The optimization process, and the streamlining of workflow can improve efficiency, and the allocation of resources. Meanwhile, the supply chain management enables SMEs to have better co-ordinations with their suppliers and vendors so as to ensure that the product flow is not interrupted until it reaches end users. Delivery disruptions can be detrimental to the business; hence automation is vital as it helps to track the products in real time while enhancing the communication between manufacturers, suppliers, distributors, and retailers. It also coordinates delivery.

Real-time inventory tracking can minimize the issue of overstocking, and the replenishing of stocks when needed. The Just in Time approach can be utilized, coupled with the digitalization of inventory management. In the business world, marketing is an inevitable part of business which requires digitization to be able to connect with customers. Meantime, SMEs need to create their own online presence so as to increase visibility and competitiveness. The standardization of brand images across all social media platforms also needs to be maintained. Evidently, businesses need to leverage on search engine optimizations and social media marketing analytics and tools if they desire to enhance customers' experience. Moreover, digitization can increase customer traffic, and subsequently, the conversion rate achieved due to the marketing strategies applied.

The transformation of online presence enhanced search engine optimization, web optimization, social media engagement, and personalization message. These efforts resonate with the target market(s), resulting in higher traffic to both online and offline stores. In line with that, customer service landscapes have also evolved due to technological advancements such that omni-channels and virtual agents can offer users a seamless experience. It seems apparent that technology allows customers to interact in multiple channels without any hassle; this allows SMEs to improve their services at any touchpoints, with the help of chatbots and virtual assistance. Moreover, personalized CRM can boost customer satisfaction and loyalty. For additional enhancement, businesses' accounting and finance areas can be digitalized by using cloud-based software that provides access to financial information in real time. This technology reduces the reliance on human support as well as data security risk.

3. CASE STUDY: EXAMPLE OF MALAYSIAN SMEs EMBRACING DIGITAL TRANSFORMATION: KHAIRUL AMIN KAMARULZAMAN @ KHAIRUL AMING

The contributions of SMEs to the Malaysian GDP growth are undeniable with many successful stories worth sharing. As an example, a former oil and gas engineer, Khairul Amin Kamarulzaman also known as Khairul Aming is one of the many social media creators of food contents, during the COVID-19 pandemic. As a result of his signature condiment called 'Sambal Nyet', he eventually became a social media influencer and entrepreneur. His transformation as an individual and as an entrepreneur has inspired many potential entrepreneurs. His videos about cooking became viral, and he gained many followers during the pandemic. He uploaded the videos and recipes onto Facebook (Rasapop) on a daily basis, during the fasting month in 2020 (Sabrina, 2023). As a result, his followers on Instagram increased from 800 to 2.8 million in 2022 (Mathan, 2022).

Khairul Aming utilized the social media platform to promote his first product back in 2021. His active online presence and his personal brand image had boosted the sales of the condiment he created. At the initial stage, his products only amounted to 200 bottles with eight employees, but today, it has increased to 5,000 bottles. About 10,000 bottles were sold in the first 50 minutes of the launch on the e-commerce site (Mathan, 2022). In 2023, Khairul Aming was able to hit MYR20 million in sales for his first product.

Early this year, Khairul Aming launched his second product, 'Dendeng Nyet Berapi' on TikTok Shop's live stream (Zikri, 2024). The Star (2024, February 3) reported that 80,000 units amounting to MYR1.2 million sales were recorded in less than four minutes on TikTok Shop which garnered 3.3 million views. The seller's online presence was eminent, and it helped to increase the product's awareness and brand visibility. To create higher customer engagement, he waited for 200,000 people to join the live session before he launched the second product. Leveraging on social media platforms such as Shopee and TikTok Shop, the seller was able to garner the attention of many people. This also helped him to promote the product to the audience.

The seller's innovativeness in terms of understanding the needs and wants of his customers enabled him to achieve success today. However, credit must also be given to the research and development efforts taken to produce the two products (Khalid, 2024). Needless to say, the automated machine provided by technology enabled him to sell his products at an affordable price despite the hike of raw materials price. This helped to reduce production costs and eventually allowed him to achieve economies of scale (Zikri, 2024). The persistence in maintaining the quality of the products over the years had also escalated customer trust (Khalid, 2024).

Khairul Aming, who is also known as the 'Sambal King' opted to sell his products online, mainly on TikTok Shops instead of physical stores. He found that managing a single channel allowed him to operate resourcefully, especially in terms of capital, logistics, and supply chain. It was estimated that TikTok Shops had generated at least 70% of his income (Zikri, 2024). Livestreaming is a very popular approach used in China, and this was similarly applied by Khairul Aming in Malaysia. In 2023, he won the Creator of the Year Award from TikTok Awards Malaysia, and in 2024, he was also awarded the Best Customer Service and Best New Seller by Shopee.

Factors supporting him include successful crisis management coupled with prompt response and swift action (WargaBiz, 2024). He engaged the social media to address any packaging or counterfeit product issues. This provided his customers with transparency which in turn, benefitted the brand image. This shows that a good organization culture is vital for business growth and employees. In addition, providing a high sense of belongingness also helped to create a positive impact such that it enhanced employees' productivity. This also added to the aspect of value co-creation. Khairul Aming is known as a kind entrepreneur who pays attention to his employees' well-being. He was often praised for his management skills and for treating his employees well by giving them allowances and free vacations (Sabrina, 2023).

Khairul Aming's popularity and influence are growing at a tremendous rate; the ingredients of his products are often sold out whenever he posts a new cooking related video. Many had decided to try out his recipe instead of buying a similar product at the Ramadan bazaar during the fasting month, due to the dissatisfaction with food quality and prices (Najihah, 2024) in the latter case. The shift in consumer behaviour reflects the degree of influence the entrepreneur has on them even though this comes with a hefty price. 'The Khairul Aming Effect' requires him to maintain a positive image (Luqman, 2004; Thirunamakarasu, 2023) and be a good example for the rest of his followers, especially the younger generation who are keen in being influencers rather than being academically inclined. Nonetheless, Khairul Aming had advised his followers on the importance of completing education first so as to be 'quality content creators'. In this regard, it can be seen that being socially responsible is a necessity for those who can influence and inspire others.

3.1. The Lessons Learned and Best Practices

With a fraction of the cost, SMEs can leverage on social platforms to create contents, promote products/services, and sell these simultaneously. By being consistent and persistent, it appears that Khairul Aming was able to build his group of followers besides building confidence and trust over time. His personality also resonated with many Malaysians who were from similar backgrounds; they cherished his success since they had been following him on various social media platforms, such as Facebook, Instagram, and Twitter. Many loved his simple cooking videos, and this has led to high customer engagement due to the comments and reposts incurred. Clearly, relationship building is essential for creating loyal followers, and a broad customer base because this cannot be achieved overnight even if something has gone viral out of the blues. One-hit-wonder would not last if nothing is being done to the low retention rate. Thus, customer building and relationship management are essential for any business.

Khairul Aming can manage the high sales volume by just relying on social media and e-commerce at the moment. This means that the need for physical retail stores is not necessary since it incurs high operation costs, high transportation costs, and high logistics costs, all of which would eventually be transferred to the customers in the form of higher price paid. E-commerce analytics, if generated, would be able to provide Khairul Aming with the trend of buying, especially in the shift of customer behaviour, sales data, and future demands. All these metrics can help him to understand his customers better, develop relevant marketing strategies, and scale up his business. Based on this information, he can make business improvements in terms of production efficiency. The right marketing analytical tools would help him to reach the right audience with the relevant message. Nonetheless, Khairul Aming needs to accelerate his efforts in maintaining and improving the product, the packaging, and the delivery quality so as to ensure customer satisfaction and hence sustainability of his business.

Based on the discussion, it seems obvious that product development and product innovation have to be monitored constantly if the producer desires to expand his products range to his customers. One way of doing so is to develop a high co-creation value by getting customer feedback and suggestions on his products. This can also boost brand attachment. Thus far, the 'Made in Malaysia' label was an advantage that gave him an edge, given that there were boycotts of foreign brands associated with Israel. In a nutshell, it can be concluded that providing good quality products and excellent customer service can boost the sales of local Malaysian products and enhance customers' lifetime values.

4. CHAPTER SUMMARY

This chapter has talked about the evolving business landscape of Malaysia which had compelled many physically based businesses to move towards virtual business. Some of them may have transitioned during the pandemic while others are currently struggling to stay competitive. Even though the digitalization rate among SMEs in Malaysia may be considered low, the government is equally, trying its best to encourage SMEs to move towards digitalization transformation. Businesses can participate by considering technology adoption in important areas of business functions. Although financial resources and digital literacy may hinder technology adoption, it can certainly be overcome through the help of government soft loans, and various learning and training activities. As a start, SME owners must acquire the right set of knowledge and skills in order to stay relevant. This is because operating a business in the digital age has to be accompanied by digitization.

Business strategies must be integrated with AI and machine learning so as to understand the shift in consumer behaviour so as to serve them better. Businesses must also be aware of technical glitches, security compliance, cybersecurity risks like data breaches, and ransomware attacks. Businesses also need to assess the importance of digitization and its extent so as to ensure that the integration between old and new systems is seamless. Businesses can start their technology adoption by making small changes instead of engaging in costly rapid transformations. Overall, this chapter highlighted that the digitalization of businesses is inevitable; thus it is timely for all SMEs to make extra efforts towards embracing the change within the changing world.

REFERENCES

Alias, N. A. B., Zi-Hao, Y., Ghazali, M. A-. F. B. M., Kang, F. Y., & Kanapathipillai, K. (2022). Factors that impact the effectiveness of social media as a marketing tool in small and medium-sized enterprises in Selangor, Malaysia. *European Journal of Management and Marketing Studies*, 7(4), 214–246.

Azalea, A., & Nehru, V. (2024, July 10). Are Malaysian SMEs falling behind in the digital age? *The Malaysian Reserve*. Retrieved from https://themalaysianreserve.com/2024/07/10/are-malaysian-smes-falling-behind-in-the-digital-age/

Banerjee, A. (2018). Chapter three – Blockchain technology: Supply chain insights from ERP. *Advances in Computer*, *111*, 69–98.

Bernama. (2020, March 18). *Malaysia's Covid-19 crisis sees 30% jump in delivery orders*. Free Malaysia Today.com. https://www.freemalaysiatoday.com/category/leisure/2020/03/18/malaysias-covid-19-crisis-sees-30-jump-in-delivery-orders/

Borah, S., Kama, C., Raksit, S., & Vajjhala, N. R. (2022). Applications of artificial intelligence in small- and medium-sized enterprises (SMEs). In P. K. Mallick, A. K. Bhoi, P. Barsocchi, V. H. C. de Albuquerque (Eds.), *Cognitive informatics and soft computing, lecture notes in networks and systems* (Lecture Notes in Networks and Systems, Vol. 375, pp. 61–70). Springer. https:// doi.org/10.1007/978-981-16-8763-1_5

Brynjolfsson, E., & McAfee, A. (2014). *The second machine age*. WW Norton & Company.

Buer, S-. V., Semini, M., Strandhagen, J. O., & Sgarbossa, F. (2021). The complementary effect of lean manufacturing and digitalisation on operational performance. *International Journal of Production Research*, 59(7), 1976–1992.

Burton, N., & Schlieman, T. (2021). User response to extended reality sponsorship activations on social media: Exploring impressions of GoPro's use of 360° video in marketing. *Journal of Interactive Advertising*, *21*(2), 75–78.

Cotteleer, M., & Sniderman, B. (2017). *Forces of change: Industry 4.0*. Deloitte Insights.

Deniz, F. (2021). Strategies for digital transformation in business. In K. Sandhu (Ed.), *Disruptive technology and digital transformation for business and government* (pp. 153–171). IGI Global Scientific Publishing.

Dimitrova, R., Rasheva-Yordanova, K., & Iliev, I. (2024). Marketing 4.0: Opportunities and challenges of extended reality marketing. In *47th MIPRO ICT and electronics convention (MIPRO)*. IEEE Explore. https://ieeexplore.ieee.org/abstract/document/10569665/authors#authors

Dutta, P., Choi, T-S., Somani, S., & Butala, R. (2020). Blockchain technology in supply chain operations: Applications, challenges and research opportunities. *Transportation Research Part E: Logistics and Transportation Review*, *142*, 102067.

Feroz, A., Zo, H., & Chiravuri, A. (2021). Digital transformation and environmental sustainability: A review and research agenda. *Sustainability*, *13*(3), 1530.

Garamendi-Colos, V., Cano-Lazarte, M., Mamani-Macedo, N., Raymundo, C., & Dominguez, F. (2020). Agile inventory management model under a digital transformation approach for stockout reduction in chemical industry's MSE. In *Proceedings of the 9th international conference on operations research and enterprise systems* (pp. 455–461).

Goyat, R., Kumar, G., Rai, M. K., & Saha, R. (2019). Implications of blockchain technology in supply chain management. *Journal of System and Management Sciences*, 9(3), 92–103.

Hasbolah, F., Rosli, M. H., Hamzah, H., Omar, S. A., & Bhuiyan, A. B. (2021). The digital accounting entrepreneurship competency for sustainable performance of the rural micro, small and medium enterprises (MSMES): An empirical review. *International Journal of Small and Medium Enterprises*, *4*(1), 12–25.

Hassan, S. H., Mohamed, N. A., & Ahmad, N. H. (2019). Social customer relationship management (s-CRM) among small- and medium-sized enterprises (SMEs) in Malaysia. *International Journal of Ethics and Systems*, *35*(1), 284–302.

Horváth, D., & Szabó, R. Z. (2019). Driving forces and barriers of Industry 4.0: Do multinational and small and medium-sized companies have equal opportunities? *Technological Forecasting and Social Change*, *146*, 119–132.

Joao Carlos, M., Silva, R., & Pereira, F. (2018). Automation technologies in small businesses: Opportunities and challenges. *International Journal of Business Automation and Digital Processes*, 6(2), 78–89.

Jing, E. (2023). *Digitalizing SMEs and industrial value chains to unlock growth for the new decade*. World Economic Forum. https://www.weforum.org/agenda/2023/06/entrepreneurs-smes-digital-transformation-amnc23/

Jurgielewicz, L. (2019). The impact of technology on business supply chain and operations: Emerging trends. *Journal of Business and Management Research*, *25*(3), 134–150.

Kagermann, H., Helbig, J., Hellinger, A., & Wahlster, W. (2013). *Recommendations for implementing the strategic initiative INDUSTRIE 4.0: Final report of the Industrie 4.0 Working Group*. Acatech.

Kee, D. M. H., Cordova, M., & Khin, S. (2023). The key enablers of SMEs readiness in Industry 4.0: A case of Malaysia. *International Journal of Emerging Markets* , 1746-8809. https://doi.org/10.1108/ijoem-08-2021-1291.

Khalid, I. (2024). *Here is what makes Khairul Aming a successful Malaysian entrepreneur*. Muslim Insiders Chamber of Commerce. https://musliminsiders.com/here-is-what-makes-khairul-aming-a-successful-malaysian-entrepreneur/

Khin, S., & Hung, W. T. (2022). Contextual impacts on industrial processes brought by the digital transformation of manufacturing: A systematic review. *Sustainability*, *11*(3), Article 891.

Khin, S., & Kee, D. M. H. (2022). Identifying the driving and moderating factors of Malaysian SMEs' readiness for Industry 4.0. *International Journal of Computer Integrated Manufacturing*, *35*(7), 761–779.

Kshetri, N. (2018). 1 Blockchain's roles in meeting key supply chain management objectives. *International Journal of Information Management*, *39*, 80–89.

Luqman, N. (2004, April 4). *Khairul Aming wins hearts of netizens by treating 100 of his workers to a raya bonus & shopping spree*. Myc.my. https://www.myc.my/articles/3413/khairul-aming-wins-hearts-of-netizens-by-treating-100-of-his-workers-to-a-raya-bonus-and-shopping-spree

Marr, B. (2016, April 5). Why everyone must get ready for 4th industrial revolution. *Forbes*. https://www.forbes.com/sites/bernardmarr/2018/08/13/the-4th-industrial-revolution-is-here-are-you-ready/

Mathan, Y. (2022). *The inspiring story of Khairul Aming: RM14 million sales for "sambal". Citizens Journal.* https://cj.my/123160/the-inspiring-story-of-khairul-aming-rm14-million-sales-for-sambal/

Meltwater. (2024). *Social media statistics for Malaysia.* https://www.meltwater.com/en/blog/social-media-statistics-malaysia

Menon, S., & Shah, S. (2019). *An overview of digitalisation in conventional supply chain management.* MATEC Web of Conferences, 292, Article 01013. In *23rd International Conference on Circuits, Systems, Communications and Computers* (CSCC 2019). Section Circuits and Systems. https://www.matec-conferences.org/articles/matecconf/abs/2019/41/matecconf_cscc2019_01013/matecconf_cscc2019_01013.html

Morakanyane, R., Grace, A., & O'Reilly, P. (2017, June 18–21). *Conceptualizing digital transformation in business organizations: a systematic review of literature. Digital transformation – From connecting things to transforming our lives.* 30th Bled eConference Digital Transformation, Bled, Slovenia.

Moro, C., Birt, J., Stromberga, Z., Phelps, C., Clark, J., Glasziou, P., & Scott, A. M. (2020). Virtual and augmented reality enhancements to medical and science student physiology and anatomy test performance: A systematic review and meta-analysis. *Anatomical Sciences Education*, *14*, 368–376.

Najihah, F. N. (2024). *#NSTviral: Khairul Aming sparks home cooking trend amidst dissatisfaction with Ramadan bazaar foods.* https://api.nst.com.my/authors/fatin-nurul-najihah

Nurzafirah, Z., Asmaai, M., Saban, A., & Saban, S. M. (2022). Impact of digitalization and analytical skill on management accounting practice in small and medium enterprise in Malaysia: A conceptual framework. *Science, Education and Innovation in the Context of Modern Problems*, *5*(4), 137–143.

OECD. (2019). Strengthening SMEs and Entrepreneurship for Productivity and Inclusive Growth: OECD 2018 Ministerial Conference on SMEs, OECD Studies on SMEs and Entrepreneurship, OECD Publishing, Paris. https://www.oecd.org/en/publications/strengthening-smes-and-entrepreneurship-for-productivity-and-inclusive-growth_c19b6f97-en/full-report.html

Pan, G., & Lee, B. (2020). Leveraging digital technology to transform accounting function: Case study of a SME. *International Journal of Accounting and Financial Reporting*, *10*(2), 24–38.

PayPal. (2022). *Accelerating SME digitalisation in Malaysia.* Newsroom. https://newsroom.apac.paypal-corp.com/stories?item=91

Pessot, E., Zangiacomi, A., & Sacco, M. (2023). Exploring SMEs innovation paths with augmented and virtual reality technologies. *European Journal of Innovation Management*, 1460-1060. https://www.emerald.com/insight/content/doi/10.1108/EJIM-02-2023-0118/full/html.

Przychocka, I., & Sikorski, M. (2024). Revolutionizing SME management: The digital transformation of financial operations. *European Research Studies Journal*, *27*(2), 78–85.

Ratnasingam, J., Khoo, A., Jegatheswaran, R., Kasim, A., Ramage, M., & Amir, M. A. (2020). How are small and medium enterprises in Malaysia's furniture industry coping with the COVID-19 pandemic? Early evidences from a survey and recommendations for policymakers. *BioResources*, *15*(3), 5951–5964.

Razak, S. A., Latip, N. S. M., & Adam, A. (2023). Social media usage and its impact on brand equity among SMEs in Malaysia. *Journal of Academia*, *11*(2), 148–160.

Sabrina, S. (2023). *7 things that prove why Khairul Aming deserves his success as an influencer & entrepreneur. Vulcan Post*. https://vulcanpost.com/828439/khairul-aming-popular-food-influencer-entrepreneur-malaysia-reasons/

Santani, S. J. (2024). Businesses, public must share burden of making Malaysia more competitive: Samenta. *The New Straits Times*. https://www.nst.com.my/business/corporate/2024/06/1068253/businesses-public-must-share-burden-making-malaysia-more

Sharma, S., Singh, G., Islam, N., & Dhir, A. (2022). Why do SMEs adopt artificial intelligence-based chatbots? *IIEEE Transactions on Engineering Management,* University of Exeter, *71*, 1773-1786. https://ore.exeter.ac.uk/repository/bitstream/handle/10871/130742/IEEE%20TEM%20accepted%20paper_Prof%20Nazrul%20Islam.pdf?sequence=1

Silva, V. L. D., Kovaleski, J. L., Pagani, R. N., Silva, J. D. M., & Corsi, A. (2020). Implementation of industry 4.0 concept in companies: Empirical evidence. *International Journal of Computer Integrated Manufacturing*, *33*(4), 325–342.

Sundblad, W. (2018). *Beyond digital transformation: How Industry 4.0 benefits your customers, employees, and culture*. https://www.forbes.com/sites/willemsundbladeurope/2018/10/03/beyond-digital-transformation-how-industry-4-0-benefits-your-customers-employees-and-culture/#55c2247c29fc

Tong, A., & Gong, R. (2020, October 20). The impact of COVID-19 on SME digitalisation in Malaysia. *LSE Southeast Asia Blog*. https://blogs.lse.ac.uk/seac/2020/10/20/the-impact-of-covid-19-on-sme-digitalisation-in-malaysia/

The Star. (2024, February 3). *Hot sales: 'Sambal King' Khairul Aming sells RM1.2mil worth of 'dendeng' in just three minutes*. https://www.thestar.com.my/news/nation/2024/02/03/hot-sales-039sambal-king039-khairul-aming-sells-rm12mil-worth-of-039dendeng039-in-just-three-minutes

Thirunamakarasu, P. (2023, April 3). *Khairulaming shares weight loss journey after doctor calls him out for using too much oil*. Says.com. https://says.com/my/news/khairul-aming-shares-weight-loss-journey-after-doctor-calls-him-out-for-using-too-much-oil

Tsang, Y. P., Yang, T., Chen, Z. S., Wu, C. H., & Tan, K. H. (2022). How is extended reality bridging human and cyber-physical systems in the IoT-empowered logistics and supply chain management? *Internet of Things*, *20*, 100623.

Ulas, D. (2019). Digital transformation process and SMEs. *Procedia Computer Science*, *158*, 662–671.

Vaghefi, N., & Jo-yee, Y. (2021). *Helping SMEs rise to challenges posed by the Covid-19 pandemic. Analysing Penang, Malaysia and the Region*. Penang Institute Issue. https://penanginstitute.org/wp-content/uploads/2021/03/Helping-SMEs-Rise-to-Challenges-Posed-by-the-Covid-19-Pandemic.pdf

WargaBiz. (2024). *Let's decode the biz strategy of Malaysia's sambal King, Khairul Aming*. https://wargabiz.com.my/2024/02/06/sambal-king-of-msia-khairul-aming-copy-his-biz-strategy/

Warner, K., & Wäger, M. (2019). Building dynamic capabilities for digital transformation: An ongoing process of strategic renewal. *Long Range Planning*, *52*(3), 326–349.

Winarsih, M., & Buyong, S.Z. (2020, August 27). MSME's performance – In the effect of accounting digitization. *ICIC 2020: Proceedings of the 1st international conference on Islamic civilization*, Semarang, Indonesia.

Zikri, A. (2024). Following success of Sambal Nyet, local online entrepreneur Khairul Aming launches second product today. *Malay Mail*. https://www.malaymail.com/news/life/2024/02/02/following-success-of-sambal-nyet-local-online-entrepreneur-khairul-aming-launches-second-product-today/115928#google_vignette

Ziółkowska, M. J. (2021). Digital transformation and marketing activities in small and medium-sized enterprises. *Sustainability*, *13*(5), 2512.

4

DIGITAL TRANSFORMATION ISSUES AND CHALLENGES: SOLUTIONS FOR MALAYSIAN SMEs

ABSTRACT

Digital transformation provides various benefits to small and medium-sized enterprises (SMEs). However, the statistics shows the implementation of digitalization is still low among Malaysian SMEs due to significant hurdles. In this chapter, we will explore the various challenges faced by Malaysian SMEs while embracing digital transformation. Financial constraints and a lack of robust information technology (IT) infrastructure can make acquiring the necessary technology a challenge. Several factors are adding to these challenges alongside limited financial resources, like lack of expertise, as SMEs may have insufficient technical expertise for the effective selection, implementation, and management of new technologies. The digital skills gap, highlighting the lack of necessary digital skills among employees, hinders the effective implementation and use of technologies to their full potential. Furthermore, recruiting and retaining competent IT specialists with expertise in digital transformation can be difficult and costly. Employees' mindsets, resistance to change within the workforce, clinging to traditional methods, and uncertainty slow down the adoption too. The impact of the digital divide among firms and its influence on SMEs' digital transformation will be further discussed in this chapter. The cybersecurity issues and several other issues that are hindering Malaysian SMEs' digital transformation initiatives are also discussed. Most importantly, the chapter discusses appropriate solutions to overcome those challenges. Taken together, this chapter aims to provide guidance to Malaysian SMEs to plan and support a smooth digital transformation journey.

Keywords: Cybersecurity, digital transformation challenges; digital skills; digital divide; financial limitations; solutions

1. INTRODUCTION

As discussed in the earlier chapters, innovation and digital revolution are transforming today's business landscape and environment. These changes can impact SMEs significantly. The rapid improvement of technology has made it necessary for the world to change, and with the occurrence of the 2019 pandemic, business environments have no choice but to succumb to the inevitable changes brought on by technology. While large organizations are taking the necessary measures to be on par with the digital transformation, it is more challenging for SMEs to navigate. There are numerous benefits to be attained from digital transformation. They include opportunities to expand into new markets, attract clients from local and global regions, access to better and more efficient client services, and the market to produce innovative goods and services that can satisfy customer needs.

Digital transformation offers SMEs with the means to compete effectively, operate efficiently, innovate continuously, and the ease to adapt to changes. By carefully adopting technology, SMEs can realize their potentials and achieve success in the digital era. Undoubtedly, digital transformation is empowered by developments in generative artificial intelligence (AI). These help both large organizations and SMEs to transform. Nevertheless, the rapid and remarkable development of digitalization has put the pressure on SMEs to conform fast, or they would be left behind (Ammeran et al., 2023).

In an economic survey conducted by the OECD in 2021, it was found that Malaysian SMEs were lagging behind larger firms in technology usage in their businesses. The limited use of technology led to a reduced output which ultimately leads to production inefficiency. The same survey also noted that if SMEs do not adopt digital transformation, they may fall behind their competitors who have been effectively using digital technologies to upgrade their services.

The chairman of the Small and Medium Enterprises Association (Samenta), Datuk William Ng, highlighted some statistics posed by the outcome of a survey with Affin bank in July 2022 which indicated that nearly 21.7% of SMEs in Malaysia have not implemented any form of digitalization in their businesses while 48.1% of SMEs are still at the early stage of digital transformation. This suggests that an average of 70% of SMEs are either at the early stage of transformation, or they have not digitized their businesses yet (Suhaidi, 2022). The report added that the implementation of digitalization among Malaysian SMEs is still very low. This chapter will thus explore the various challenges faced by SMEs in embracing digital transformation so as to offer them several possible solutions for practical application.

2. DIGITAL TRANSFORMATION CHALLENGES

2.1. Financial Limitations

Similar to any form of change that can affect an industry, digital transformation in the Malaysian context can also affect the local industry of SMEs, thereby incapacitating their participation in the digital economy. One of the main challenges faced by SMEs is the high cost of adoption and implementation. It appears that SMEs are challenged by the limited financial resources available for them to adopt new technologies. While it is true that there has been a rise in SMEs' adoption of digital technologies, many of them are facing issues in trying to survive in this competitive landscape.

Limited financial resources prevent SMEs from possessing and recruiting adequate technological expertise to assist them in digital transformation. Accordingly, they lack the confidence to apply any form of selection, implementation, and management of these new technologies effectively. Tham Lih Chung, the Chief Executive Officer of Incite Innovations Group had spoken exclusively with *Business Today* regarding the forces that can propel SME growth (BusinessToday, 2024). He noted that there is a possible incompatibility between the new technology and the extant infrastructure. This implies that companies need to invest more funds for an upgrade. The World Economic Forum (2021) had also emphasized that implementing new technologies would require modifications to infrastructure, and this can be expensive and time-consuming for SMEs.

Despite the growing demands, many SMEs face obstacles in implementing essential technologies for long-term competitiveness. SMEs also need to ensure their consumers and suppliers are prepared to embrace the new technologies. This means that market readiness for new technology has to be in place prior to its implementation. Moreover, the cost of implementing the latest technology and infrastructure within the business environment can be high. The SMEs Corporation Malaysia noted that about 69.7% of Malaysia's firms are micro firms (Department of Statistics Malaysia (DOSM), 2023) that operate with limited R&D funds, revenue, or even sales that must be secured and prioritized before they can enhance and implement the system for their internal or external use. Most Malaysian SMEs do not have any investment plan to spend on IT resources and capabilities. Consequently, local SMEs choose to stay in the 'comfort zone', given their existing resources.

Solutions: The lack of financial resources poses a significant challenge to digital transformation, not only in Malaysia but also in countries around the world. To overcome this issue, most countries have implemented several funding opportunities to support SMEs. For instance, Irish government, as part of the National Digital Strategy, offers a Trading Online Voucher Scheme to small businesses with limited or no e-commerce presence, specifically those with 10 or fewer employees and a turnover of less than EUR 2 million. This scheme supports small businesses with grants of up to EUR 2,500 to help them develop e-commerce or online trading platforms (Dreyer & Nygaard, 2020). Whereas in Japan, the SME Productivity Revolution Promotion Project provides various subsidies to firms, including an IT introduction subsidy. As part of this IT introduction subsidy, small businesses can receive up to 4.5 million yen for IT-related projects, in addition to computers and hardware leasing costs (Dreyer & Nygaard, 2020).

Similarly, the Hong Kong government provides financial assistance to SMEs, particularly in purchasing new IT equipment and online digital solutions, to enhance productivity. On the other hand, Singapore supports SMEs' digital transformation in several ways. The government provides funding of SGD 300 per month for five months to microenterprises, such as hawker centres, coffee shops, wet markets, etc., to adopt cashless e-payment platforms. Additionally, under the SME Go Digital programme, a Digital Resilience Bonus of up to SGD 5,000 is available for SMEs adopting new technology. Food and beverage companies that have already implemented e-commerce technologies and are looking to adopt advanced technologies are eligible for financial assistance of SGD 5,000 (Dreyer & Nygaard, 2020)

Similar to the aforementioned countries, the Malaysian government also offers multiple financing options for SMEs. For instance, Bank Negara Malaysia (BNM) provides a range of funding options, including the Skim Pembiayaan Mikro, the Micro Enterprises Facility, and the All Economic Sectors Facility. Both the Skim Pembiayaan Mikro and the Micro Enterprise Facility provide financing of up to RM 50,000 to microenterprises, gig workers on digital platforms, and self-employed individuals in an easy, fast, and convenient manner, without requiring collateral (Microfinance – Bank Negara Malaysia, 2024).

In July 2023, there was an outstanding SME financing of RM368 billion mentioned in BNM's database. To date, BNM has given RM600 million to SMEs such as the micro, small, and medium enterprises (MSMEs), under the BNM's *Belanjawan* 2024 scheme (Bank Negara Malaysia, 2023). This scheme involves raising allocations for the Micro Enterprises Facility, and the All-Economic Sectors Facility as a step towards assisting small contractors and microentrepreneurs.

Another possible solution for SMEs is the availability of collaboration strategies in Malaysia. The government establishes strategic collaborations between SMEs and larger enterprises. One example of such a project is the Export Acceleration Mission (EAM) to Dubai which is coordinated by the Malaysia External Trade Development Corporation (MATRADE), in partnership with the Ministry of Entrepreneur Development and Cooperatives (KUSKOP), with SME Banks. The collaboration took place in February 2024 and it seeks to enable Malaysian SMEs to expand into international markets by forming relationships with influential customers, especially those in the Middle East and North African (MENA) region (MATRADE, 2024).

In line with this, on 23 January 2024, *Bursa* Malaysia developed the SME X Platform which was partnered with the Companies Commission of Malaysia (SSM). This platform aims to assist SMEs in raising funds for their development and commercial expansion by linking them with capital resources like private equity firms, venture capitalists, or other financial institutions (Bursa Malaysia, 2024). Therefore, it is important for Malaysian SMEs to explore the funding sources discussed above to address their financial limitations. They may also consider alternative financing options such as government loans, community development financial institutions, and crowdfunding platforms (The MSME, 2023). These funding opportunities provide chances for Malaysian SMEs to collaborate with larger corporations, granting them access to new markets and additional funding sources to expand and digitalize their businesses.

2.2. Lack of Digital Skills

Within the digital age, the success of SMEs is largely dependent on their skilled workforce. Their knowledge releases the full potential of the emerging technology, converting investments into observable gains like heightened efficiency, and a competitive advantage. Their capacity to adjust and generate fresh concepts propels innovation and expansion, thereby thrusting the enterprise into the future. An efficient business is closely related to the business' effectiveness in managing its resources and in streamlining its operations. It is thus their expertise and abilities that would enable these SMEs to deliver outstanding client services and to promote contentment and allegiance.

When companies invest in advanced technologies, employees need to possess sufficient knowledge and the capacity to use these technologies effectively so as to improve productivity. In reality, however, the existing workforce is not equipped with adequate digital skills that can take them through the digital transformation shift. Evidently, an inadequacy of proficiency in digital abilities among employees can impede the successful implementation and utilization of new technology. Furthermore, recruiting and retaining competent IT specialists with expertise in digital transformation can be difficult and costly. Companies may have a very good system or an app in the latest technologies, but without the digitally skilled employees to use and implement these technologies, firms' investment in these technologies would still be a waste. It appears that the digital skill gap in Malaysian SMEs is still an alarming issue. The section below offers several suggestions to minimize this digital skill gap.

Solutions: Based on the above discussion, it is clear that SMEs need to have the right talent pool in order to utilize the system to its full benefits. A few solutions were identified. One of them is for the government to encourage collaborations between large and small enterprises as well as between government and private sectors – public-private-partnership (PPP) as a means to develop training programmes. This exercise can help employees to familiarize themselves with new technologies, hence making them more knowledgeable in this sector. The government can also develop upskilling programmes for employees while also enhancing national development policies that focus on spreading digitalization nationwide. As an illustration, the initiative 'MyDigital' can be proposed since its main aim is to transform Malaysia into a digital economy powerhouse. For this purpose, the Malaysian Digital Economy Blueprint which is a roadmap to achieve the goal of MyDigital was created. The blueprint contains three phases: Phase 1 (2021–2022) focusses on strengthening the foundation of digital use, Phase 2 (2023–2025) drives digital transformation and inclusion, and Phase 3 (2026–2030) positions Malaysia as a regional leader in digital content and cybersecurity.

Another initiative is the Upskill Malaysia programme created for individuals to enhance their professional skills. The programme offers a wide range of courses and resources. An additional likelihood is Digital UP by Malaysia Digital Economy Corporation (MDEC) Sdn Bhd which was set up to train professionals so as to enable them to adapt to the rapidly changing digital economy (MyGOV, 2024). A further possibility is to offer complementary investments in skill development for non-ICT specialists. This exercise could raise awareness as well as boost employees' active participation in digital transformation. With the knowledge or expertise gained, organizations could overcome the obstacles and barriers hindering digital transformation. All these could impact the long-term digital viability of SMEs. A more in-depth discussion on digital skills development can be found in Chapter 5, where we explore the specific skills needed for SMEs to thrive in the digital landscape.

2.3. Resistance of Employees to Change

Even though it is inevitable, the process of digitalization for businesses could adversely affect the staff or management, such as employees having a strong resistance towards the adoption of new technologies and information systems. It is also possible that staff may be unwilling to work out of their comfort zone because they lack the awareness, knowledge, expertise, and confidence in using the new technology implemented by their company (Ammeran et al., 2023).

An article in *Business Today* in November 2021 highlighted that digital growth incurs extra operational costs. Financial losses may also occur due to the improper use of technology. The improper use of technology may be due to the wrong selection of technology and lack of skills among employees in using the latest technologies. This could cause SMEs to fall behind others with regard to most current business trends besides competitiveness in newer and larger markets. Inadvertently, this could also lead to customer dissatisfaction and a drop in clients or sales (BusinessToday, 2021). Many SMEs in the micro and small category also asserted that their staff were reluctant to adopt the new technology due to their lack of knowledge but there were also some outstanding employees who chose to self-learn these new technologies by watching online videos while also asking the IT person or helpdesk to solve their doubts/issues.

Solutions: To resolve these issues highlighted above, the management has to take more active roles by constantly motivating and supervising their staff towards adopting and using the technology properly. This is because the incorrect use of technology could lead to other issues such as inaccurate data or missing sales records which could cause poor decision-making (UOB Business Insights, 2023). To resolve employees' reluctance to embrace digital technologies in their workplace, various approaches can be applied. First, the leaders or owners of the enterprises must actively support digital transformation. They should make efforts to act as a role model for their staff. For instance, they could take the lead to try using the new technology on their own so as to demonstrate to the subordinates on how to participate actively. They should communicate to the staff as to why their business process needs to be managed differently, and what benefits employees can reap from the technology.

Furthermore, management needs to provide proper training to staff and also to give them adequate timeframe to learn the necessary digital skills. To motivate employees, companies can choose to reward staffs who had learned the technologies efficiently, and also applied this knowledge in their work. All these suggestions could create a more conducive environment for employees to feel comfortable with the new technology.

2.4. Digital Divide Among Firms

The digital divide is prevalent, particularly among Malaysian firms when digital transformation is in process. The COVID-19 pandemic acted as the accelerator for firms to implement digitalization, especially during the period of lockdown restrictions. As a result, many companies began to invest in digital solutions or become involved in digital transformation. However, not all Malaysian companies were able to do so because of the digital divide prevailing among large and SME firms. Well-established and large corporations with more extensive resources were able to implement specific technology, but SMEs were at a disadvantage. Particularly, larger firms were able to have access to the latest and most advanced of technological resources whereas SMEs were digitally passive due to limited resources.

Another observed disparity is the gap between the former and the latter in collecting high quality data. Large organizations were predisposed to better advantages such as collecting huge amounts of data, storing these in high capacity cloud based servers, investing in data mining projects, use the latest AI and machine learning to build models, analyse data, do predictions and forecasts, and use advanced analytics for making efficient and timely decisions so as to gain commercial value from the data. In contrast, SMEs were deprived of such access to huge amounts of data; they were also unable to reap the above-mentioned benefits. Consequently, the whole debilitating issues demotivated SMEs from progressing in the digitalization landscape.

Solution: Several initiatives have been taken by the Malaysian government to close the digital divide among firms. One such initiative was the Smart Automation Grant introduced in December 2020 (Malaysian Investment Development Authority (MIDA), 2020a, 2020b). This programme offered financial help to eligible SMEs to invest in automation solutions. It was hoped that this could, to some extent, narrow the digital divide between large firms and SMEs. The proposed solution includes robotics, process automation, Internet of Things (IoT), and AI technology. The principal goal of this Smart Automation Grant is to speed up SMEs' adoption of smart technology. The grant had hoped to improve operational efficiency, lower expenses, and increase overall production. It was thought that by automating repetitive procedures, SMEs can free up human resources who can then focus on strategic initiatives as well as decision-making process.

Undoubtedly, automation streamlines procedures, lowers human errors, and accelerates operations. Thus, SMEs which have implemented smart automation are expected to be more competitive in the marketplace. Rather than threat to job opportunities, automation frequently results in the development of new roles, particularly in technological industries. During a health crisis (such as the COVID-19 pandemic), automated systems had enabled company continuity. Initiatives such as MyDigital consist of plans aimed at accelerating digital transformation in all industries; it includes initiatives aimed at closing the digital gap. Another programme is the National Policy on Industry 4.0, known as Industry 4WRD. Its main goal is to improve digitalization within the manufacturing sector as well as the services associated with it, especially among SMEs. The government is currently encouraging SMEs to participate in digital transformation programmes which give access to learning opportunities, industry experts' exposure, and contacts with IT service providers (UOB Business Insights, 2023).

Bridging the digital divide between large corporations and SMEs requires the collaborative efforts of all stakeholders. This was also emphasized by the Davos Agenda 2023 which stated that collaborative partnerships between large corporations, SMEs, and government bodies need to be encouraged. Collaborative projects may concentrate on offering support, training, and digital infrastructure (World Economic Forum, 2023a, 2023b). This is because collaborative projects can enhance knowledge exchange, and promote mentorship where large corporations lend their resources, skills, and technological expertise to SMEs. This practice could further add value to SMEs in fields like social media management, data analytics, and e-commerce. Furthermore, large companies can host webinars or seminars to encourage interactions and the exchange of ideas. They can also offer resources such as trends, consumer information, and market insights to SMEs. These resources could support SMEs in making wise judgements and informed decisions.

2.5. Cybersecurity Issues

Cybersecurity is the biggest concern in today's business world. The 2020–2024 report on the Malaysia Cyber Security Strategy stated that cyber threats are likely to cause the loss of RM 51 billion to the country (Malaysian Investment Development Authority (MIDA), 2023), if not duly addressed. There are five core pillars, 12 strategies, and 35 action plans which outline the nation's cybersecurity agenda. This includes legislative initiatives such as the Cybersecurity Bill, capacity building for cybersecurity professionals, fostering of public–private collaborations, and improving international relations (OpenGov Asia, 2024).

Malaysia recently suffered from several cyberattacks (The Edge Malaysia, 2022) while LGMS Bhd's report related to cybersecurity ratings in November 2022 highlighted that nearly 18 companies listed on the main board of Kuala Lumpur Stock Exchange had suffered from active cyberattacks in terms of malware infections in just one month. Data leaks affected around 478 companies, and databases of seven companies were exposed. Remote Desktop Protocol was exposed to about 37 companies. This suggests that users from any part of the world can access and control a computer. It was also noted that about seven companies had an issue with remote sync whereby such software tool files could be easily transferred to a remote server (NST Business, 2022). These are alarming incidents emphasizing on the rise of cyberattacks in recent years. If this is the case with public listed companies, SMEs with low investments in cybersecurity software and tools may face even more serious consequences.

It appears that cybercriminals target SMEs three times more than the large corporations counterpart because SMEs are especially vulnerable to ransomware attacks. Even tiny amounts of ransom can have a significant impact on their small business margins (The Sun, 2023). After the COVID-19 pandemic, many companies began implementing the 'work from home' setting for a few days in a week; they also adapted the 'Bring Your Own Device (BYOD)' policy, a practice which had accelerated cases of cyberthreat events even more because the system and data were exposed and compromised.

To date, many SMEs have not digitalized their operations, neither have they conducted their IT health check frequently, nor even attempted to implement cybersecurity measures. In this regard, SMEs were thus more vulnerable to cyberattacks. Therefore, it is important that companies have an effective cybersecurity implementation. Digital transformation involves automation which includes storing sensitive and confidential data. This means that SMEs need to have strong cybersecurity measures at every stage of the data exchange.

Solutions: The Malaysia Cyber Security Strategy (2020–2024) that was published by the Malaysian government outlines tactics for safeguarding companies against cyberattacks (OpenGov Asia, 2024). These were developed for the purpose of assisting SMEs in protecting their digital assets, helping

SMEs in conducting and disseminating best practices, enabling SMEs to create awareness, and offering them resources in light of COVID-19 pandemic's increased use of remote work, and other BYOD policies.

With the advent of new technology, SMEs thus face more challenges. In particular, they need to know what measures to adopt in order to strengthen their cybersecurity position. There are two-pronged approaches. Firstly, SMEs need to organize regular trainings. They also need to create more awareness programmes that can empower employees in identifying potential cyberattacks, and reacting to them effectively. Secondly, SMEs need to invest in essential cybersecurity tools and software so as to augment their overall security system. Such an investment can be optimized by exploring government grants or external financing options which can be found on the official websites of the Malaysian Investment Development Authority. Thirdly, SMEs can define more precise procedures for handling cyber incidents so as to reduce harm and to expedite recovery. Other measures are for SMEs to conduct regular IT health checks, take data protection measures, and enforce strict access controls.

The Kaspersky Financial Threat Report (2021) had noted that cybercriminal organizations like Zbot, SpyEye, CliptoShuffler, and Emotet are prevalent and targeting small and vulnerable firms. Although SMEs are the government's focus in digital transformation, 47% of them have trouble raising funds to strengthen their cyber risk defences (BusinessToday, 2022). Therefore, collaborations with cybersecurity experts have to be fortified so that SMEs can stay up to date and protect sensitive information. Through these collaborations, the SMEs can benefit from the guidance of cybersecurity experts in drafting security and data protection policies that are safe for use and include access controls. These policies must be adhered to in order to promote strong security. Cybersecurity experts can also offer SMEs threat intelligence feeds that can enable the latter to remain alert to new dangers.

2.6. Digital Transformation Journey: Steep Learning Curve for SMEs

The digital transformation journey is indeed a steep learning curve for SMEs. SME's digital transformation is a paradigm shift which offers three promises – enhanced productivity, improved efficiency, and greater competitiveness. The rapid changing business landscape is nonetheless causing SMEs significant problems. The first issue is shifting viewpoints and approaches. The acceptance of digital transformation is dependent on changes which include employees. As discussed earlier in Section 2.3, employees may be struggling with shifting their traditional mindset and methods to adopting an innovative and tech-dependent culture. These employees who had been ingrained in the traditional ways may be resistant to the new ways of working. They may be less open to experimentation, adaptability, and continuous learning. This can cause the shift from analogue to digital to become a tough battle.

Another issue is responding to evolving demands. Due to the scarcity of resources, the practice of updating and integrating the most recent technology developments for their companies may be difficult. SMEs are likely to face a shortage of skilled professionals who can implement new technologies effectively. Meanwhile, inadequate cloud computing capacity can also restrict SMEs' operational flexibility and scalability because storing and managing vast volumes of data are critical, especially for making informed decisions and providing individualized customer service.

Solutions: To make it easier for employees to adapt, change their perspectives, and be open towards digital transformation, stakeholders and the management team need to provide strong support. This is because digital transformation involves not just IT but also other aspects including employees. Therefore, it is important for SMEs to develop micro-sized learning programmes which can be integrated with traditional methods to make employees learn, understand and manage the systems easily. Furthermore, the employees should be encouraged to use the open source platforms and online learning resources which are arguably free of charge or at low cost with faster and more convenient forms of learning. With this, SMEs are better equipped to change the views of their employees, and also their approach towards change. In this regard, SME owners should strive to use the most impactful digital tools and train the employees in using these tools effectively. This is better than pressuring the employees to learn everything perfectly. Making an investment in agile learning can transform to a long-term benefit for SMEs, particularly when executed through experimenting and learning new technologies. This approach is more likely to encourage employees to learn and adapt quickly.

According to Flat Rock Technology (2023), one way of overcoming these challenges is to have a fundamental shift in perspective and approach. SMEs must understand how critical it is to stay up to date with the demands of innovation and technology. The World Economic Forum (2023a, 2023b) had noted that for SMEs to survive and prosper, they must keep up with innovation and technology. It was observed that even if SMEs understood the importance of being on par with innovation and technology, an additional issue was the scarcity of resources. The technology suppliers now offer additional services, such as continuous maintenance and updates. SMEs can then utilize these tools to stay informed about the new features and functionalities of technology.

A final measure to resolve the issues would be for SMEs to adopt an agile mindset which is to permit their employees to experiment with new concepts, and for the management to view failure as a way of achieving success.

2.7. Wide Technology Options and Issues with Third-party Digital Platforms

The huge amount of accessible technology and digital platforms can easily overwhelm SMEs because 'choice overload' can pose various challenges. For instance, there are difficulties in choosing the right platform and option since all these platforms contain diverse features. This makes it difficult for SMEs to identify the substance that is most relevant to their needs and budgets. Moreover, inadequate technical expertise can cause the evaluation of complex technology to be difficult, thus it is not possible to predict how, and in what way these platforms would adapt and grow with businesses.

An additional problem is related to the platform fees and the sharing of private company information with matching algorithms. SMEs have no control in this process (OECD, 2021). It, therefore, makes it difficult for SMEs to integrate the different technologies and platforms as integrating several systems is costly and time consuming for SMEs. In addition, different platforms impose different subscription fees thus SMEs need to have the budget to address the various subscription fees, and other costs incurred for implementation, training, and maintenance. In this regard, policymakers need to create a conducive digital environment that can support SMEs in leveraging these platforms effectively.

Other issues include the dangers associated with potential lock-in effects, competition distortion, and digital security. For instance, a lock-in effect can occur when SMEs become highly dependent on a particular platform. When all customer data, product information, and sales have been integrated into one platform, it can be impossible to switch to another. This becomes more complicated should the platform be an extensive one which also offers unique features. Since this can also be crucial for SMEs' operations, looking for an alternative can be difficult. Lock-in effect limits their innovative business minds because there are certain processes that some platforms expect SMEs to strictly adhere to. In this situation, dominant platform providers have the leverage to raise prices while SMEs have limited bargaining power to negotiate terms.

An additional issue is competition distortion which is caused by network effects, data advantage, and limited visibility. Since popular platforms have an ever-growing user base, they tend to have the upper hand in most situations such as the advantage of having vast amounts of user data. SMEs may also struggle to gain visibility on large, competitive platforms due to this gap. This, therefore, widens the gap between large and small competitors.

The final issue related to digital transformation adoption is the problem of digital security for SMEs, particularly those using third-party services. These platforms may be breaching data security by revealing sensitive information, such as client details and financial data. Linked to this is the ambiguous data security standards offered by these platforms which make it difficult for SMEs to comply with data protection laws. Since SMEs have minimal control over the security mechanisms, they are forced to rely on the platform provider's standards. Taken together, there is a substantial digital security problem faced by SMEs who are navigating the world of digital platforms.

Solutions: To overcome these issues, SMEs must make proper selections and planning. Firstly, they need to conduct a need assessment by defining their business goals. Then, they need to find out the most appropriate functionality needed for their business operations, followed by evaluating and comparing the platforms based on individual objectives, prices, and future expansion needs. Platforms that make use of open data standards should be given priority since they facilitate a smoother transfer of data should they ever need to switch providers.

The next important step is for SMEs to make consolidations. Instead of using individual sets of incompatible solutions, they should aim for a consolidated technology stack with a few well-integrated platforms. They also need to look for a managed service provider so as to save time, and to release their internal resources. Finally, SMEs should emphasize on data protection and security. There should be contracts with clearly defined data ownership and guidelines on how they will handle it with platforms. They should also consider implementing additional security measures beyond what is offered by the platforms. SMEs could use a mixture of solutions provided by different providers for specific needs, thereby minimizing the lock-in effects. Additionally, SMEs can look into open-source software solutions before making decisions. Open-source platforms offer more control and flexibility than commercial solutions, thereby allowing SMEs to tailor to their exact requirements.

2.8. Inadequate E-commerce Adoption by SMEs

Nonetheless, even with the potential advantages of e-commerce, SMEs frequently encounter difficulties in their adoption of e-commerce. Salah and

Ayyash (2024) had mentioned a variety of factors that can influence SME entrepreneurs' decision to adopt e-commerce. They include trade partner readiness, perceived service quality, consumer readiness, perceived trust, current circumstances, social influence, perceived ease of use, perceived usefulness, individual differences factor, and competitive pressure. Other factors affecting SMEs' e-commerce adoption are the lack of digital skills, the requirement to modify business models, the cost of platform structures, the disclosure of private company information, dangers associated with digital security, the distorting of competitions, and potential lock-in effects.

While large enterprises keep adopting advanced tools so as to expand their market, SMEs are adhering to their basic offerings which are preventing sales. E-commerce is a necessity for SMEs because it offers a bigger geographical coverage and a larger clientele base. Without it, SMEs are restricted due to their lack of exposure, and their limited market reach. With e-commerce, particularly, SMEs could have access to platforms that offer online shopping with round-the-clock accessibility, and easier online transactions (OECD, 2021). E-commerce also simplifies marketing and sales procedures such as order handling, inventory control, and marketing. Without it, SMEs need to rely on traditional procedures which are relatively slow and fallible.

Solutions: To facilitate e-commerce adoption, firstly poor communications infrastructure needs to be addressed. This includes improving network systems, bandwidth, and internet penetration so as to reach more people reliably. To develop confidence among early adopters, it is important to solve the poor e-commerce security system, and the telecommunications infrastructure. This means that IT professionals have to be sourced and trained while security systems need to be improved. The industry's CEO or management team must have the mindset of wanting to embrace new technologies, and new ways of conducting businesses while the technology vendors must be able to provide adequate services and assistance.

It has been noted by the Malaysian Investment Development Authority (MIDA, 2022) that the government has offered extensive initiatives and programmes to help micro small and medium enterprises (MSMEs) to begin their e-commerce journey. The MDEC had also executed the Go-eCommerce Onboarding and Shop Malaysia Online campaigns under Belanjawan 2021 as a step in encouraging the adoption of e-commerce and e-payments. As of 31 December 2021, both campaigns have successfully benefitted more than 830,000 MSMEs, with 365,900 new MSMEs coming onboard. Through collaborations between 32 e-commerce and e-payment partners with MDEC, these MSMEs have collectively generated RM7.39 billion in income. This implies that there can be future partnerships with e-commerce platforms so as to provide SMEs with a larger customer base as well as to improve logistics such as quick doorstep delivery. Today, the norm is prompt delivery services including daily services which are backed by added conveniences such as tracking and notifications.

In today's e-commerce landscape, businesses need to start simple, and be user-friendly. Their expansion can be accelerated by offering a small product selection on an easy-to-use platform. To uncover their target audience, and to modify their e-commerce plans appropriately, SMEs have to do market research. To get in front of the target market, they could use emails and social media. To get past financial struggles, they could use open-source platforms that emphasize natural expansion. Although open source platforms need some technical expertise, it is the most economical way to initiate.

SMEs can use free web tools and guidance from well-established companies to develop skills and support. Furthermore, the government can create and offer online training programmes to teach SMEs the essential skills needed to operate on e-commerce platforms. Skills like digital marketing and website management can empower SMEs to start online stores. On the customer side, to develop loyalty and trust, SMEs should improve and prioritize their customer service. They can also integrate reviews into their online systems based on market needs to increase sales. These strategies can help SMEs realize the enormous potential of online sales. Since SMEs differ in nature, they encounter various obstacles; thus, their strategies to promote e-commerce adoption should be tailored to meet their specific needs and demands.

3. ARE WE REALLY GOING GREEN WITH DIGITAL TRANSFORMATION?

The digital transformation holds great promises for businesses to attain those objectives related to environmental sustainability. This is because the environmental effects of digital transformation can be both beneficial and negative. While digital transformation can help to ensure environmental sustainability, it has to be approached with a sustainable mindset. This involves addressing the negative environmental consequences caused by digital technologies, and their supply chains (UNEP – UN Environment Programme, 2024).

Truong (2022) emphasized that these environmental effects have implications on the digital products' resources and energy, such as ICT device manufacture, energy consumption, and electronic waste disposal. For instance, the mining and exploitation of natural resources used for the manufacture of hardware items cause resource depletion and global warming. This is compounded by the extraction and mining operations of raw materials including heavy metal emissions, acidification, and pollution of groundwater and water supplies. Other direct environmental implications include the improper method of collecting, recycling, and disposing of electrical and electronic equipment.

Finally, the greenhouse gas emissions caused by the usage of electricity and the disposal of waste water could also harm biodiversity. Anyhow, it can be said that green innovation is the way forward since it has the potential to minimize pollution and improve the environment. It is the fundamental technique for integrating economic growth with environmental improvement (Wang et al., 2022). Digitalization boosts productivity, decreases energy intensity, and promotes economic growth, but it relies largely on huge amounts of data which indirectly, increases energy consumption and digital equipment (Akberdina et al., 2024).

The MIT technology review conducted in 2022, in association with InvestKL, was meant to encourage digital transformation in Malaysia while also maintaining sustainability. As the main commercial hub of Malaysia, the city of Kuala Lumpur had also implemented a comprehensive smart city plan which was aimed at accelerating digital transformation. Its main emphasis was to promote education on cloud technologies and AI. In its 2022 Budget, the Malaysian government had prioritized technology investment by allocating a maximum of MYR100 million (US$23.7 million) in grants for smart automation and a minimum of MYR30 billion (US$7 billion) for government-affiliated companies to invest in renewable energy, supply-chain modernization, and 5G infrastructure.

It also encouraged partnerships with technology companies and Global technology and mobility corporations. One of these, Microsoft and Socar from Korea had made investments and extended their operations to Kuala Lumpur, with a special focus on green innovation and business prospects (MIT Technology Review, 2022). These projects encouraged businesses to adopt digital changes as well as make considerations for environmental protection. It is inevitable that the digital transformation in which the country aspires for could contribute to climate issues, if it is not managed with care. Due to this possibility, it is worth giving some attention to these plans meant for digital change by ensuring that they include a focus on using environmental friendly methods. Companies which prioritize sustainability should also include efficient digital solutions. This is because the future of businesses would be led by such companies that prioritize the environment and use efficient digital solutions.

4. CHAPTER SUMMARY

This chapter has discussed the various challenges and issues associated with digital transformation that are faced by Malaysian SMEs. The discussion had noted that the lack of finances is SMEs' biggest challenge when striving to adopt digital transformation. The next challenge is their lack of digital skills within the industry. Although it is necessary to implement new technologies at the workplace, employees may feel threatened due to their lack of knowledge about the new system. They become resistant to the change due to the assumption that new technologies may alter the existing workflow and process and they are expected to put in additional efforts to learn and to adjust to the new environment. An additional challenge is the issue of digital divide among firms in terms of access to infrastructure and resources may slowdown the process of digital transformation among the SMEs.

Cybersecurity issues are another impending factor since SMEs may find it difficult to bounce back if they get affected by cyberattacks. This chapter also highlighted the issue of adaptation and the right coping mechanism caused by the steep learning curve. SMEs also faced difficulties in identifying the right technologies to implement. The issue of compatibility and integration with third-party platforms was also presented. This was followed by a discussion on the syndrome of low adoption of e-commerce among Malaysian SMEs. Finally, this chapter dwelt on the environmental issues that may arise due to digital transformation. Several solutions for SMEs were also provided as guidelines.

REFERENCES

Akberdina, V., Kuzmin, E., Kyriakopoulos, G. L., & Kumar, V. (2024). Editorial: Sustainability of digital transformation for the environment. *Frontiers in Environmental Science*, *12*, 1371047. https://doi.org/10.3389/FENVS.2024.1371047/BIBTEX

Ammeran, M. Y., Noor, S., & Yusof, M. (2023). Digital transformation of Malaysian small and medium-sized enterprises: A review and research direction. *Lecture Notes in Networks and Systems*, *488*, 255–278. https://doi.org/10.1007/978-3-031-08090-6_16

Bank Negara Malaysia. (2023). Financing for small and medium enterprises (SMEs). https://www.bnm.gov.my/sme-financing

Bursa Malaysia. (2024). *Media release Bursa Malaysia launches SME X platform in collaboration with Companies Commission of Malaysia to facilitate fundraising for SMEs.* http://bit.ly/SMEXVideo

BusinessToday. (2021). *77 percent of Malaysian SMEs stuck in early stages of digitalisation.* https://www.businesstoday.com.my/2021/11/11/77-percent-of-malaysian-smes-stuck-in-early-stages-of-digitalisation/

BusinessToday. (2022). *Cybersecurity remains key to digital transformation and adoption in Malaysia SMEs.* Retrieved April 29, 2024, from https://www.businesstoday.com.my/2022/07/25/cybersecurity-remains-key-to-digital-transformation-and-adoption-in-malaysia-smes/

BusinessToday. (2024). *Malaysia SMEs are trailing behind riddled with productivity challenges compared global counterparts.* https://www.businesstoday.com.my/2024/01/21/malaysia-smes-are-trailing-behind-riddled-with-productivity-challenges-compared-global-counterparts/

Department of Statistics Malaysia (DOSM). (2023). Profile and performance of MSME in 2023. https://www.smecorp.gov.my/index.php/en/policies/2020-02-11-08-01-24/sme-statistics

Digital Sustainability in 2024: Importance & Top 5 Digital Solutions. (2024). https://research.aimultiple.com/digital-transformation-and-sustainability/

Dreyer, M., & Nygaard, K. (2020, June 15). *Governments encourage SMEs to adopt new technologies.* https://som.yale.edu/blog/governments-encourage-smes-to-adopt-new-technology

Flat Rock Technology. (2023). *Turn challenges to opportunities: SMEs in digital transformation.* https://flatrocktech.com/blog/the-challenge-of-digital-transformation-for-smes

Kaspersky financial threat report. (2021). *Securelist.* https://securelist.com/financial-cyberthreats-in-2021/105898/

Malaysian Investment Development Authority (MIDA). (2020a). Managing cybersecurity challenges in pursuit of digital transformation. https://www.mida.gov.my/mida-news/managing-cybersecurity-challenges-in-pursuit-of-digital-transformation/

Malaysian Investment Development Authority (MIDA). (2020b). *Smart Automation Grant (SAG) to enable future-proofing of local businesses.* https://www.mida.gov.my/media-release/smart-automation-grant-sag-to-enable-future-proofing-of-local-businesses/

Malaysian Investment Development Authority (MIDA). (2022). *E-commerce: The digital heart of Malaysia's economy.* Retrieved May 1, 2024, from https://www.mida.gov.my/mida-news/e-commerce-the-digital-heart-of-malaysias-economy/

MATRADE. (2024). Empowering Malaysian SMEs through continuous strategic collaboration among agencies. Retrieved April 29, 2024, from https://www.matrade.gov.my/en/about-matrade/media/press-releases/press-release-2024/6025-empowering-malaysian-smes-through-continuous-strategic-collaboration-among-agencies

Microfinance – Bank Negara Malaysia. (2024). https://www.bnm.gov.my/microfinance

MIT Technology Review. (2022). *Breaking new ground: Sustainability in Malaysia.* https://www.technologyreview.com/2022/07/15/1056027/breaking-new-ground-sustainability-in-malaysia/

MyGOV. (2024). Capacities for Digital Transformation | Industry4WRD: National Policy on Industry 4.0 | MyDigital and 4iR. https://www.malaysia.gov.my/portal/content/31187

NST Business. (2022). 18 Bursa main board-listed companies had active malware infections in November. https://www.nst.com.my/business/2022/12/859284/18-bursa-main-board-listed-companies-had-active-malware-infections-november

OECD. (2021). *SMEs going digital: Policy challenges and recommendations.* https://www.oecd.org/digital/smes-going-digital-c91088a4-en.htm

OpenGov Asia. (2024). *Empowering cybersecurity: Malaysia's digital safety bill.* https://opengovasia.com/2024/03/14/empowering-cybersecurity-malaysias-digital-safety-bill/

Salah, O. H., & Ayyash, M. M. (2024). E-commerce adoption by SMEs and its effect on marketing performance: An extended of TOE framework with AI integration, innovation culture, and customer tech-savviness. *Journal of Open Innovation: Technology, Market, and Complexity*, *10*(1), 100183. https://doi.org/10.1016/J.JOITMC.2023.100183

Selangor Journal. (2021). Malaysia digital economy blueprint identifies issues, challenges. https://selangorjournal.my/2021/02/malaysia-digital-economy-blueprint-identifies-issues-challenges/

SMEs in the online platform economy. (2021). The Digital Transformation of SMEs. *OECD iLibrary.* https://www.oecd-ilibrary.org/industry-and-services/the-digital-transformation-of-smes_1386638a-en

Suhaidi, N. (2022, November 24). *Online competitiveness among SMEs delayed by digital gap, cost.* https://themalaysianreserve.com/2022/11/24/online-competitiveness-among-smes-delayed-by-digital-gap-cost/

The Edge Malaysia. (2022). *Managing cybersecurity challenges in pursuit of digital transformation.* https://theedgemalaysia.com/node/650395

The MSME. (2023). *Overcoming key challenges faced by MSMEs: Strategies and solutions.* https://blog.themsme.com/2023/02/05/overcoming-key-challenges-faced-by-msmes-strategies-and-solutions/#google_vignette

The Sun. (2023). *SMEs advised to install cyber security systems.* https://thesun.my/local_news/smes-advised-to-install-cyber-security-systems-PM11489886

Truong, T. C. (2022). The impact of digital transformation on environmental sustainability. *Advances in Multimedia, 2022*(1), 6324325. https://doi.org/10.1155/2022/6324325

UNEP – UN Environment Programme. (2024). Digital transformations. Retrieved April 29, 2024, from https://www.unep.org/topics/digital-transformations

UOB Business Insights. (2023). Bridging digital divide among Malaysian SMEs. https://www.uob.com.my/business/sme-hub/insights/bridging-digital-divide.page

Wang, L., Liu, S., & Xiong, W. (2022). The impact of digital transformation on corporate environment performance: Evidence from China. *International Journal of Environmental Research and Public Health*, *19*(19), 12846. https://doi.org/10.3390/ijerph191912846

World Economic Forum. (2021). *Pandemic drives need for technology adoption among SMEs but barriers remain > Press releases.* https://www.weforum.org/press/2021/12/pandemic-drives-need-for-technology-among-smes-but-barriers-remain/

World Economic Forum. (2023a). Digital transformation can unlock SME potential. https://www.weforum.org/agenda/2023/07/digital-transformation-potential-smes/

World Economic Forum. (2023b). *Here's how we can work together to bridge the digital divide.* https://www.weforum.org/agenda/2023/01/here-s-how-work together-bridge-digital-divide-davos2023/

5

NURTURING FUTURE WORKFORCE: ENHANCING SME's READINESS FOR DIGITAL TRANSFORMATION IN MALAYSIA

ABSTRACT

As artificial intelligence (AI), big data, and the diverse interconnected systems transform the operations of industries worldwide, a significant mismatch between the skills taught by educational institutions and those demanded by the labour market emerges. In view of the urgency to close the gap resulted from digital transformation, this chapter thus delves into the challenges faced by industries in Malaysia. Particularly, it looks at how local institutions can bridge such gaps on one hand; while it also discusses how industries in Malaysia can remain competitive before discussing the skills new graduates and the existing workforce need to acquire on the other hand. The discussion will thus emphasize on technical skills, such as AI, data science, and cybersecurity, alongside employability skills, such as critical thinking, communication, and problem-solving. The chapter then examines the role of government interventions, including Malaysia's Technical and Vocational Education and Training (TVET) programmes and other global skill-development initiatives in addressing the skills gap. The role of small and medium enterprises (SMEs), which often struggle to provide adequate training opportunities, is also accounted for. It focusses on government programmes which are aimed at supporting workforce development. To foster a future-proof workforce, this chapter then calls for a stronger alignment between educational curricula, industry needs, and government policies. By promoting digital competencies and lifelong learning, nations can be assured that their economies are being well-protected so that they can all thrive in the evolving global landscape driven by the Fourth Industrial Revolution (IR 4.0) technologies.

Keywords: Labour market; digital transformation; workforce; Malaysia's Technical and Vocational Education and Training programme; workforce development

1. INTRODUCTION

The IR 4.0 and the rapid development of digital technologies have led to many transformative changes. These are taking place very rapidly across various sectors of businesses. Technological advancements are affecting the nature of science and innovation which requires a workforce that is adept in AI, big data, blockchain, interconnected networks, and high-speed computing to help drive new discoveries and innovative productions (Sajitha et al., 2021). These have also affected the social, ecological, and economic landscape of the world significantly. They have reshaped the workforce which now requires staff who are highly skilled specialists equipped with precise knowledge, logical thinking, and strong communication and collaboration abilities. Our current workforce is, however, less than expectation in itself for this shift because the country barely foresees the urgency of technological advancements, and the readiness and skills required for workers to adapt to a fast-changing work environment. This highlights the wide digital skills gap as one of the challenges (as stated in Chapter 4) hindering the digital transformation of SMEs. This chapter henceforth, delves into this specific issue in detail.

Technological advancement is seen in many aspects of the world. To be able to manage these technologies, the current workforce needs to have higher levels of education, better aspects of professionalism, and higher levels of competencies – absorptive capabilities, especially the young labours. They need to be better equipped for employability, thus they would need higher digital skills – the ability to handle and manage and also adopt those new technologies. One of the programmes offered by the Malaysian government as a measure to cater for this issue is the upskilling and retraining programmes for the existing workforce. It is a vital step for safeguarding the business industry in this new and digital era.

The skills required by the labour market to stay competitive are rapidly evolving due to technological innovations. However, not everyone is susceptible to these changes, and the benefits they offer. Low-skilled employees are the group that is most sceptical of automation. They tend to be reluctant to adapt to changes. Due to this matter, they become the category of employees who would most be required to become adept with technology and the new skills and knowledge needed. This also applies to old-school professionals who had been on the work scene for too long. With industries in the country majority being composed of SMEs, and manpower running them being highly old-schooled in thoughts and mindset, these SMEs are therefore facing challenge of reskilling, upskilling, and adopting a new learning approach. In this regard, they also become the essential workforce for development.

The 2023 Digital Skills Gap Report, highlighted by Wiley, had indicated that over 40% of the respondents surveyed, was detected three critical in-demand skills lacking in their respective organizations. They encompass strategic thinking and analytics (46%), digital communications (41%), and project management skills (40%). The lack of these three skills in the workforce places many businesses at a competitive disadvantage, exacerbating the process for them to bridge the gaps between their employees' current capabilities and the skills required to succeed in the digital economy. Likewise, Microsoft discovered that 65% of the managers hired by companies identified the difficulty of finding qualified digital talents. This is further endorsed by the Gallup and Amazon Web Service which showed that only 11% of the workers in the United Kingdom were equipped with the required digital skills.

It is crucial for industries to understand the specific skills and capabilities required, for the sake of addressing the technical issues that may emerge. Research has revealed this pervasive gap between employers and employees. There is an urgent need to address this mismatch, particularly between the industry and academia.

A recent study looking at Malaysian employees found that 65% of them stated that digital skills are essential for today's workforce (Economist Impact, 2023). In fact, with new technologies, the demand for technical skills has escalated in Malaysia. The Malaysia Digital Economy Corporation predicted that there will be a growth of 7.6% for IT professionals over the next three years. Today, basic digital skills are indispensable as noted by 83.1% of Malaysian employees while 49%aware of the need for more advanced competencies like data analysis, and 47.7%stressed the need to enhance digital marketing (Economist Impact, 2023).

In relation to the wide skills gap occurring in this country, it is the SMEs in Malaysia that are affected seriously. They lack skilled and technical expertise. They remain ignorant and tend to stress less on upgrading the skills and knowledge of their workforce. They are sometimes hesitant in participating in the government-sponsored training programmes (Musa & Chinniah, 2016).

As a result, they also encounter other challenges in attracting and retaining highly qualified personnel with relevant skills. Consequently, they struggle in looking for the right workers with the desired expertise (HRDF, 2020).

2. DIGITAL TRANSFORMATION AND SKILL REQUIREMENTS

As mentioned before, digital transformation is reshaping the business and workforce landscape. Technological advancement has become a primary focus for industries as well as in research and development. While much attention has been paid to the benefits of the technological advent, little focus has been given to the role of human factors, particularly issues like workforce capabilities, training, development, and leadership. History has always reflected that people tend to focus on technological changes first before they take into account the effort to train the individuals who can use these technologies in the future. This delay often results in a gap between the introduction of new technologies, and the availability of a prepaid workforce. When those companies or individuals fail to update their knowledge, they get left behind.

The technological skills required by industries can be classified into three: emerging, evolving, and expiring skills. Emerging skills are driven by technological advancements, such as AI, blockchain, machine learning, and internet of things. They require the newest competencies. Evolving skills are capability to adapt as market needs change, with companies striving to stay efficient and competitive by adopting more advanced technologies. Expiring skills are skills that become obsolete as technology replaces certain jobs and performs certain tasks more efficiently than human being.

The IR 4.0 is expected to affect all professions, and groups of people, particularly youths, recent graduates, and those just entering the workforce. Evidence suggests that while many traditional jobs will disappear, new jobs would be created by technology. Many young people get left behind as these new roles require new skills which they do not have (Kassid, 2022). Inevitably, those with lower skills may have fewer job options. This can affect those youths who lack education access and background, employment, and training. Consequently, they could be pushed to insecure, low-paying jobs with undesirable working conditions.

A mismatch between the supply and demand for professional workers may arise, resulting in a paradox where there is a high demand for employees with specific skills, yet high unemployment persists due to an unskilled workforce in general. This imbalance causes significant challenges for industries that face labour shortage. Simultaneously, many people may be struggling to look for suitable employment. To avoid such a scenario, workers need to adapt by learning and applying new skills and knowledge. This adaptation requires both short- and long-term planning by the government. Meantime, close collaborations between the educational institutions and the industry need to be revived. Their collaborations can help them to identify the competencies and skills needed in response to technological changes and labour market challenges.

Without proper planning and strong connection between education, businesses, and the labour market, issues like unemployability become exacerbated. Many countries face problems, such as an influx of overqualified tertiary graduates, job mismatches, and long-term unemployment (Vasileiadou, 2023). Overqualified employees who are often young and lack the necessary skills and experience, are at risk of economic and social difficulties, such as receiving lower wages or being unable to find suitable jobs. Inadequate job-related training would further compound these problems causing a rise in unemployment or job insecurity, especially following technological changes (CEDEFOP, 2018; Vasileiadou, 2023).

Digital transformation requires the workforce to be equipped with the skills and knowledge that are necessary to implement and monitor technology effectively (Ghosh et al., 2022). At present, it seems that governments in developed countries, like the United States, have implemented various skills development programmes. These are done in collaboration with educational institutions, industry certifications, and apprenticeship initiatives. Such programmes would help the industries to equip their workers with the right digital skills that are essential for the industries to achieve success within a technology-driven economy. Meanwhile, these programmes can also develop a talent pool that is ready for the digital age (Ghosh et al., 2022). Like Malaysia, the African government is also prioritizing skills development and workforce preparation as a strategy to adapting herself into the digital world.

2.1. Employability and Workforce Skills

The concepts of employability and employment are often used interchangeably, yet they are distinct. Employability is a broader concept that encompasses not only the factors relevant to securing a job, but also includes those that are being prepared for work (Bikse et al., 2022; Little, 2001). Employability also looks at the qualities required to maintain employment and to progress within the workforce. They include capabilities, skills, and up-to-date knowledge in a specific area of expertise. In this sense, employability is a prerequisite for employment (Harvey, 2003; Lees, 2002). It involves equipping students with a range of knowledge, skills, and behaviours that would enable them to become successful in employment and in life, thereby preparing them for future works (Cole & Tibby, 2013).

Researchers have categorized employability skills in various ways to explain the characteristics a person should possess. Robinson (2022) proposed that employability skills are divided into three categories: basic academic skills, higher order thinking skills, and personal qualities. Other researchers like Stiwne and Alves (2010) stated that employability is comprised of four dimensions: efficacy beliefs and metacognition, subject knowledge, skilful practices, as well as procedural knowledge (Bikse et al., 2022; Stiwne & Alves, 2010). Talin (2021) identified 23 key skills required for future jobs. These can be further divided into fundamental skills that are necessary for future works, and job-specific skills which are important for addressing future complex problems that arise due to the adoption of new technology. Talin also emphasized that personal qualities can help individuals to adapt to changes smoothly over time (Bikse et al., 2022; Talin, 2021).

Other researchers have categorized skills into groups like basic skills, core skills, transferable skills, generic skills, soft skills, behavioural competencies, and cross-curricular skills (Awofala et al., 2017). McGunagle and Zizka (2020) argued that employability skills for the IR 4.0 era include Information Communication Technology (ICT) literacy, critical thinking, problem-solving, creativity, innovation, decision-making, information literacy, and collaboration (McGunagle & Zizka, 2020). Another aspect proposed by Laar et al. (2020) look at a broader set of expertise which includes seven core skills, such as information management, creativity, communication, collaboration, critical thinking, problem-solving and technical skills. Five contextual skills, such as flexibility, self-direction, lifelong learning, ethical awareness, and cultural awareness were also mentioned (Laar et al., 2017, 2020).

The above studies emphasized the need for local and foreign education systems to prepare the young people for jobs that may not yet exist, but are driven by the demands of the knowledge society (Bikse et al., 2022). In response to technological changes and labour market challenges, Bikse et al. (2022) then divided the essential key competencies and skills needed for employability into four categories. Firstly, core skills include education, lifelong learning and training, technical skills, information management, problem-solving, critical thinking, perspective-taking, communication and collaboration, and creativity skills. Another category is contextual skills that cover ethical and cultural awareness, flexibility, and self-direction. Additionally, there are social skills, which involve social awareness, response construction, empathy, social cognition, emotional labels, inhibitory control, causal understanding, and identification skills. Next, digital skills, which encompass knowledge of computers and various programmes, innovations, mathematical thinking, information searching, media understanding, and proficiency with various digital tools and applications.

With significant technological advancement, it is important for technical staffs to possess specialized skills in the area of AI, machine learning, Cybersecurity, data science, cloud computing, and blockchain. They are the skills highly on demand. Those involved with technology must also have the expertise in programming languages and tools, such as Java, Python, SQL, JavaScript, Linux, AWS, Agile project management, C/C++, software development, APIs, data analysis, and HTML5, REST, and DevOps. Evidence drawn from the industry and research further showed that certain skills including communication, leadership, teamwork, adaptability, problem-solving, time management, flexibility, and emotional intelligence are also essential across all fields. While technical skills are highly valued for the operations of technology-driven tools, non-technical skills are also crucial for success within a competitive job market. These skills are further categorized and explained in detail in the following sections.

Within the technological landscape, companies are required to use various software, specific skills, and specific knowledge to operate their businesses, depending on the nature of their respective activities. Digital skills thus act as the foundation for companies to use these technologies while more advanced professional skills are necessary at the higher levels. Table 2 illustrates examples of these platforms and the descriptions for each of these systems.

There is no doubt that today's industries require digital skills that support the use of technology. Technology enables the working individuals to effectively utilize technological tools. In turn, technology offers the means and opportunities for companies to develop and apply digital skills. It is essential for organizations, regardless of their size, to adopt some forms of technology. This makes digital skills a requirement for employability, and job security for any industry. Table 3 illustrates some examples of the relationship between digital skills and the relevant technologies.

Industries that rely heavily on Microsoft technologies to conduct various business operations would definitely need Microsoft skills that can apply the expertise to use Microsoft products and services effectively and efficiently. These would enable businesses to perform their respective tasks, communicate, collaborate, and solve arising problems. Proficiency in Microsoft word, Excel, and PowerPoint would enable employees to create, manage, and present specific documents, reports, and data with ease. Additionally, Microsoft Power BI and Excel's data

Table 2. Examples of Technology, Platform, and Skills.

Technology	Platform	Description/Skills
Customer relationship management (CRM)	For example, Salesforce, HubSpot	Familiarity with CRM platforms Data analysis and interpretation Communication skills Sales and marketing knowledge
Enterprise resource planning (ERP) systems	For example, SAP, Oracle, NetSuite	Proficiency in ERP software Understanding of business processes Data management skills Problem-solving abilities
Collaboration and communication tools	For example, Slack, Microsoft Teams, Zoom	Proficiency in communication tools Ability to collaborate remotely Time management skills Familiarity with virtual meeting etiquette
Project management software	For example, Trello, Asana, Jira	Project management expertise Organizational skills Task prioritization abilities Understanding of agile methodologies
Accounting and financial software	For example, QuickBooks, Xero	Proficiency in accounting software Financial analysis skills Understanding of accounting principles
Data analytics and business intelligence tools	For example, Tableau, Power BI	Data analysis skills Understanding of data visualization techniques Knowledge of SQL or other query languages critical thinking abilities
E-commerce platforms	For example, Shopify, WooCommerce	E-commerce platform management Digital marketing skills Understanding of online payment systems Customer service skills
E-commerce skills	Payment Gateways, Shopping Cart Software Analytics Tools, Digital Marketing Skills,	Design, develop, and manage e-commerce websites and platforms, such as online storefronts, payment systems, and inventory management
Content management systems	For example, WordPress, Joomla	Website development skills Proficiency in CMS platforms Knowledge of HTML/CSS Content creation and management abilities
Social Media Management Tools	For example, Hootsuite, Buffer	Social media marketing skills Content creation abilities Understanding of audience engagement metrics Communication skills
HR management systems	For example, BambooHR, ADP	Human resources management knowledge Understanding of HR software Interpersonal skills

Table 3. Digital Skills and Related Technologies.

Digital Skill	Examples of Related Technology	Description
Computer literacy skills	Operating Systems, Microsoft Office, Google Workspace	Proficiency in using computers Operating systems Basic software applications (e.g. Microsoft Office Suite, Google Workspace)
Data skills	Data analysis tools Databases Spreadsheets	Ability to collect, process, analyse, and communicate data using various tools and methods
Data literacy skills	Microsoft Excel Google Sheets Tableau	Ability to read, understand, analyse, and communicate data as information
Cloud skills	Amazon Web Services (AWS) Google Cloud Platform Salesforce	Cloud computing platforms Cloud storage services Understanding of cloud architecture Networking and security principles Scripting or programming skills (e.g. Python, PowerShell)
Cybersecurity skills	Antivirus software Firewalls encryption authentication	Ability to protect data, systems, and networks from cyber threats and attacks using various tools and techniques
AI skills	Machine learning Natural language processing Computer vision	Ability to leverage AI tools and solutions to automate tasks, optimize processes, and generate insights
Transversal skills	Communication tools Collaboration platforms Creativity software Problem-solving applications	Ability to communicate, collaborate, create, and solve problems using various digital tools and platforms
Data visualization	Tableau Microsoft Power BI Google Data Studio D3.js	Analysing financial data Data manipulation and financial modelling Proficient in Excel with advanced skills in functions such as VLOOKUP, PivotTables Skilled in using Tableau for data visualization SQL database management system

analysis features are crucial for executing functions involving data analysis and decision-making. The mastery of these skills, whether for basic office tasks or advanced cloud computing solutions, would equip employees with the necessary skills to fulfil their responsibilities within a wide range of industries. Table 4 illustrates some examples of Microsoft skills and the related technologies.

Table 4. Microsoft Skills and Related Technologies.

Microsoft Skill	Examples of Related Technology	Description
Office skills	Microsoft Office applications, such as Word, Excel, PowerPoint, Outlook	Ability to create, edit, and share documents, spreadsheets, presentations, and emails using Microsoft Office applications
Azure skills	Microsoft Azure cloud platform, services, and solutions, such as Azure DevOps, Azure AI, and Azure IoT	Ability to access, use, and manage Azure cloud resources and services for data and application development, deployment, and management
Dynamics 365 skills	Microsoft Dynamics 365 business applications, such as Sales, Customer Service, Finance, Supply Chain Management.	Ability to use and customize Dynamics 365 business applications to automate and optimize business processes and operations
Power Platform skills	Microsoft Power Platform tools and solutions, such as Power BI, Power Apps, Power Automate, Power Virtual Agents	Ability to use and build Power Platform tools and solutions to analyse data, create apps, automate workflows, and build chatbots
Teams skills	Microsoft Teams collaboration platform, features, and integrations, such as chat, calls, meetings, channels, apps	Ability to use and integrate Teams collaboration platform to communicate, collaborate, and coordinate with others

Communication skills facilitate the effective and efficient exchange of information, ideas, and perspectives. In the working environment, having a strong command of presentation skills is beneficial. The said skill enables staff to clearly convey their ideas and information to colleagues, clients, and stakeholders. Since part of communication is persuasion, employees would also have the ability to persuade and convince others such as clients, team members, or the management towards adopting a particular course of action or decision. This can significantly impact the company's success.

Another aspect of communication is negotiation skills which would enable employees to increase sales, enhance project management, and also the leadership competence to balance the different interests among all. This can ensure an outcome that benefits all parties. In brief, it can be deduced that the various components of communication skills which include presentation, persuasion, negotiation, active listening, and information conveying skills are fundamental for the individual's success across industries. When combined with the effective use of related technologies, these skills could further enhance the individual's ability to collaborate, influence, and perform so as to achieve positive results in the modern workplace. Table 5 highlights some examples of communication skills and the related technologies.

The information technology (IT) field focusses on technological skills as it expounds in rapid succession. Much as it is aiding businesses in automation and digitalization. The IT field is still robotic in a sense because everything that technology can do is programmed. This means that technology is still non-human and this implies that it lacks the emotional skills and soft skills offered by the human touch. Communication skills are important for the workforce so as to complement the digital world of economy. Thus, IT professionals would still need to interact with other individuals, such as their supervisors and colleagues, particularly when reporting on certain issues or when providing certain technical support. These IT workers often collaborate with other teams to work on various projects, thus their communication would also incur the use of written and verbal communications, alongside active listening skills so that they are equipped well to provide clear feedback on complex issues.

In addition, IT professionals also require strong time management skills which are especially vital when conducting assessments of project durations, task prioritization, and deadline adherence of schedules, all of which ensure

Table 5. Communication Skills and Related Technologies.

Communication Skills	Examples of Related Technology	Description
Written and oral communication	Word processors, email clients, chat apps, video conferencing tools	Ability to create, edit, and deliver messages using various written and spoken formats
Presentation	Presentation software, projectors, microphones	Ability to design and deliver engaging and informative presentations to various audiences
Active listening	Video conferencing platforms and collaboration tools (e.g. Slack, Trello); headphones, earphones, and noise-cancelling devices	Ability to pay close attention to what others are saying, ask questions, and provide feedback
Persuasion	CRM software, email marketing platforms, social media platforms, blogs, and podcasts	Ability to influence others' opinions, attitudes, and behaviours using various techniques and strategies
Negotiation	Online platforms, tools, and services for negotiation, such as Negotiatus, Negotiate, Asana, Monday.com, Slack, email	Ability to influence others' opinions, attitudes, and behaviours using various techniques and strategies

the timely delivery of projects. IT professionals frequently juggle multiple projects and responsibilities, thereby necessitating a structured approach towards achieving specific goals and delivering results.

Another potential skill required is analytical skills which are crucial for IT professionals to detect potential problems before they occur, and to analyse data so as to extract key information, such as performance indicators based on trend reviews. Creativity is an additional component because the skill could empower IT staff to develop innovative ideas and solutions for improving their work processes and/or for designing solutions to problems. This then leads to another type of skill called the problem-solving skills. They are very much needed by staff who need to know how to address challenges, troubleshoot technical issues, develop strategies for increased efficiency, and resolve conflicts among team members.

The next component is leadership skills because IT professionals must also be adept at helping others so as to enhance their productivity through the best software and technology. Leadership abilities are diverse, and they encompass matters such as task delegation, goal setting, and conflict resolution. Adaptability and quick thinking are also essential for IT workers to manage the evolving demands of businesses more effectively and efficiently. These soft skills, when combined with technical skills which include knowing how to use and manage various technologies and tools, are necessary for employability at different levels within the IT field. Table 6 lists some examples of IT and technical skills and related technologies.

Having a deep knowledge of AI technologies is essential for the modern workforce since it is one of the most transformative forces shaping the future of various industries. AI can automate routines and repetitive tasks, thereby freeing up employees to focus on higher-level work that requires critical thinking, creativity, and problem-solving. The ability to understand how to leverage AI would thus, improve operational efficiency. This then allows workers to optimize their workflow, and to boost productivity. Employees armed with the skill to use AI can design and manage systems that enhance customer satisfaction and engagement. Professionals with AI expertise can also contribute to the development of cutting-edge solutions, fostering new business opportunities, and expanding market reach. AI technology knowledge would thus equip the respective professionals to adapt to new roles, develop novel solutions, and stay relevant in an AI-driven job market. The ability to harness AI for strategic, operational, and innovative purposes is becoming a key differentiator in many industries. Table 7 presents examples of AI and the future technical trends together with the related technologies which can aid in understanding the growing importance of these skills in the modern workplace.

Table 6. IT and Technical Skills and Related Technologies.

IT and Technical Skill	Examples of Related Technology	Description
Web development	Web development tools and frameworks, such as HTML, CSS, JavaScript, React, Angular, etc.	Ability to design and build websites and web applications using various tools and frameworks
Software engineering	Software engineering tools and methodologies, such as Java, C#, Git, Agile, etc.	Ability to develop, test, and maintain software systems and applications using various tools and methodologies
Database administration	Database management systems and tools, such as SQL, Oracle, MySQL, MongoDB, etc.	Ability to create, manage, and secure databases and data using various systems and tools
Project management	Project management tools and software, such as Microsoft Project, Asana, Trello, etc.	Ability to plan, execute, and monitor projects using various tools and software
Technical support	Technical support tools and software, such as Zendesk, Freshdesk, TeamViewer, etc.	Ability to provide technical assistance and troubleshooting to customers and users using various tools and software
Programming and software development	Python, Java, JavaScript Visual Studio Code React MySQL Docker JUnit	Proficiency in programming languages relevant to the organization's tech stack Understanding of software development methodologies Knowledge of version control systems
Web development	HTML, CSS, and JavaScript WordPress, Django, React Python MySQL GitHub/GitLab/Bitbucket	Understanding of web technologies Familiarity with web development frameworks and content management systems
Database management	MySQL, PostgreSQL, MongoDB	Proficiency in database management systems Ability to design, implement, and maintain databases

3. THE MALAYSIAN WORKFORCE AND GOVERNMENT PLANS

The Malaysian Productivity Corporation's (MPC) report of 2022 emphasized the significant shortage of highly qualified human resources across industries. This issue hindered the nation's economic growth (Yunus et al., 2024). Accord-

Table 7. AI and Future Technical Trends and Related Technologies.

AI and Future Technical Trend	Examples of Related Technology	Description
Generative AI	Generative AI tools and frameworks, such as GPT-4, Gemini, ChatGPT	Ability to use and create generative AI tools and frameworks to generate text, images, audio, video, and other content
Quantum computing	Quantum computers and platforms, such as IBM Quantum, Google Quantum AI, Microsoft Azure Quantum	Ability to use and program quantum computers and platforms to perform complex calculations and simulations
Edge computing	Edge devices and networks, such as smartphones, IoT devices, edge servers	Ability to use and manage edge devices and networks to process data and run applications closer to the source
Blockchain	Blockchain platforms and applications, such as Ethereum, Bitcoin, Hyperledger	Ability to use and develop blockchain platforms and applications to enable secure, decentralized, and transparent transactions and data sharing.
Augmented reality (AR) and virtual reality (VR)	AR and VR devices and software, such as Oculus, Meta, Realeyes	Ability to use and create AR and VR devices and software to enhance or simulate reality and provide immersive experiences

ing to a 2018 Randstad study (randstad.com.my), more than 90%of Malaysian employees claimed to be illiterate in the digital skills needed for their jobs. This had led to difficulties in coping with technological demands. This skills gap contributed to the rising unemployment rate among graduates who lacked digital competencies. The Ministry of Education's (MOE) Graduate Tracer Study 2018 found that one in every five Malaysian graduates was unemployed, primarily due to the lack of digital skills. This means that employability rests on graduates possessing the right digital skills. They are the key solution to Malaysia's economic growth (Kamil et al., 2023; Malaysia Digital Economy Corporation, 2021). A report by HRD Corp further noted that there was a shortage of communication skills among Malaysia's workforce (Halili, 2021; HRDF Human Capital Report, 2019; McKinsey, 2022). The same report indicated that there was a growing need for jobs to be aligned with Industry 4.0, and this means that positions, such as data analysts, data scientists, and big data analysts (HRDF Human Capital Report, 2019; McKinsey, 2022) are very much on demand.

Despite the objectives to enhance human capital accumulation outlined in the 12th Malaysian Plan, the number of skilled workers had only increased to 29.6%as of December 2023; the statistics fall short of the 35% target identified for 2025 (MPC, 2024). These shortfalls point to the challenges of implementing the digital enhancement plans of the country. Clearly, some SMEs had failed to adopt the best management practices provided by the agencies (HRDF, 2020). This, therefore, highlights the need for immediate structural change to take place within the SMEs, including increasing the proportion of higher-skilled workers (Kamil et al., 2023).

A study by Rahmat et al. (2019) explored Malaysian university students' awareness of Industry 4.0, the importance of digital skills, and their preparedness for future careers by examining their higher critical thinking skills. The findings revealed that some students were familiar with digital skill sets, but many lacked knowledge in the essential industry skills (McKinsey, 2022; Rahmat et al., 2019). This indicates the weak connection expectation mismatch between universities and the industry. One potential way to rectify this issue is for the government to strengthen the educational institutions' awareness about the skills required to align with industry needs. This groundwork is crucial for preparing the current talent pool to adapt to new technological realities. Likewise, companies also need to assess their future workforce so that they can attract and retain skilled workers with the knowledge and expertise to work with new technologies (McKinsey, 2022).

Thus far, it appears that the Malaysian MOE recognizes the importance of developing future-proof graduates who are equipped with the right skills, abilities, and values to meet Industry 4.0 demands (moda.my.gov, 2019). The World Economic Forum (WEF) had identified 10 critical components which are essential for the future workplace. They encompass skills and areas of development like complex problem-solving, coordinating with others, critical thinking, creativity, people management, negotiation, emotional intelligence, judgement decision-making, service orientation, and cognitive flexibility (McKinsey, 2022; Rahmat et al., 2019).

The Malaysian government has thus far, prioritized the need to improve the existing workforce's readiness to succeed in a rapidly evolving work environment. It is also striving for SMEs to have access to the necessary resources and support when adopting Industry 4.0 technologies, particularly in developing a skilled workforce that is enhanced with the critical core skills required for the future workplace (Rahmat et al., 2019).

Another solution identified by the government is the TVET programme which is aimed at equipping the workforce with the essential knowledge and skills required for employment. TVET combines formal, informal, and non-formal learning methodologies to prepare young individuals for the job market (UNESCO, 2017; Yunus et al., 2024). The TVET curriculum in Malaysia has evolved in response to the country's economic growth and industrialization (Sofea, 2022). The Industry Lead Bodies regularly update the National Occupational Skills Standards so as to ensure that training remains relevant to emerging skills sectors. In tangent with this, a government-industry TVET coordination body has also been established to foster deeper collaborations between the government and industry players (Sofea, 2022; Yunus et al., 2024). TVET serves as the pathway to employment, particularly for young people; it equips graduates with market-relevant competencies (Yunus et al., 2024). These efforts demonstrate the government's commitment, alongside industry initiatives, in enhancing the workforce with the knowledge and skills necessary to adapt to technological changes and digital transformation.

3.1. SMEs in Malaysia

Unlike big corporations, SMEs often lack the knowledge and capacity to provide adequate training opportunities for their employees. But with the PENJANA (National Economic Recovery Plan) initiative, the SME Development programme is aimed at enhancing productivity and cost-effectiveness among Malaysian SMEs via functional and operational training courses. Prior to this, programmes like the SME Skills Upgrading Programme and SME Training Incentive Programmes were designed to boost the knowledge, skills, and competencies of SME employees in Malaysia.

The HRDF is only available for employers with 10 or more employees, thus many micro firms are denied the access to these training programmes. Nonetheless, some non-HRDF registered companies can still benefit from other financial incentives, such as the SME Training Incentive Programme, and other government-funded strategic initiatives. In addition to these programmes, the recognition of prior learning has been initiated to allow certified skills and knowledge to be gained formally or informally. Employers seeking recognition for their employees' skills and experiences can also obtain financial assistance through the HRDF. This can help them to increase the number of skilled workers in the national labour market.

4. CHAPTER SUMMARY

The 4IR IR 4.0 has ushered in unprecedented changes which were driven by rapid advancements in digital technologies. They help to reshape industries, and economies worldwide. Technological innovations, such as AI, machine learning, big data, and interconnected systems have taken centre stage, causing a demand for highly skilled workers. Nevertheless, there are still significant skills gap, leaving both new graduates and existing workers unprepared for the demands of the digital economy. This mismatch between the skills provided by educational institutions and the competencies sought by industries underscore the critical need for clear policy interventions.

The Malaysian government and industries must, therefore, prioritize the workforce by equipping the employees with both emerging and evolving skills so that they can remain competitive. Digital transformation demands technical expertise as well as core employability skills, such as critical thinking, communication, creativity, and problem-solving. Thus, young people entering the labour market need to have a better awareness of the skills that are most relevant to the industry in order to secure employment. This can be achieved through close collaborations between educational institutions, the government, and business industries so as to ensure that the curricula are aligned with industry needs, and that the talent pipeline is adequately prepared for future challenges.

Further to this, reskilling and upskilling programmes are essential for the existing workforce because they enable individuals to adapt to the technological shifts, thereby eliminating obsolescence. Initiatives such as the TVET, and various global skill-development programmes demonstrate the government's commitment in addressing these challenges. More concerned efforts are also required to bridge the gap between educational institutions and the industries creating employment so as to ensure that the young graduates and the current workforce are equipped with the necessary skills to thrive in the IR 4.0 era.

In conclusion, creating a future-proof workforce requires clear policies that promote skills development, industry alignment, and lifelong learning. By fostering awareness about industry demands among the youths, and empowering the current workforce with essential digital and employability skills, the country can sustain economic growth and maintain a competitive edge in the digital age. The future of the Malaysian SMEs' workforce depends on their effectiveness in addressing the digital skills gap in keeping pace with rapid technological advancements. SMEs often struggle with limited resources to provide adequate training for their employees, yet these businesses must embrace digital transformation to remain competitive. However, a greater emphasis on aligning workforce competencies with industry demands is essential. By fostering collaborations between the government, the educational institutions, and the SMEs, Malaysia can cultivate a more resilient, future-ready workforce that can navigate the challenges of IR 4.0 while also driving a sustained economic growth.

REFERENCES

Awofala, O. A., Olabiyi, O. S., Ogunleye, A., & Uchenna, N. (2017). School administrators' perceptions of the employability of preservice science, technology, and mathematics teachers through teaching practice in Nigeria. *International Journal of Educational Sciences*, 3, 42–55.

Bikse, V., Grinevica, L., Rivza, B., & Rivza, P. (2022). Consequences and challenges of the fourth industrial revolution and the impact on the development of employability skills. *Sustainability*, *14*, 6970. https://doi.org/10.3390/su14126970

Cole, D., & Tibby, M. (2013). *Defining and developing your approach to employability: A framework for higher education institutions*. Higher Education Academy.

Dhesi, D. (2023). Challenges await SMEs in shifting focus to IR 4.0. *The Star*. https://www.thestar.com.my/business/business-news/2023/02/20/challenges-await-smes-in-shifting-focus-to-ir-40

Economist Impact. (2023). Bridging the skills gap: Fuelling careers and the economy in Malaysia, Edited by Ritu Bhandari. https://impact.economist.com/perspectives/talent-education/bridging-skills-gap-fuelling-careers-and-economy-malaysia

European Center for the Development of Vocational Training (Cedefop). (2018). Insights into skill shortages and skill mismatch: learning from Cedefop's European skills and jobs survey. Luxembourg: Publications Office. Cedefop reference series; No 106. http://data.europa.eu/doi/10.2801/645011

Ghosh, S., Hughes, M., Hodgkinson, I., & Hughes, P. (2022). Digital transformation of industrial businesses: A dynamic capability approach. *Technovation*, *113*, 102414.

Halili, S. H. (2021). *Incorporating education 4.0 skills in a work-based learning environment*. https://www.bernama.com/en/thoughts/news.php?id=2037246

Harvey, L. (2003). *Transitions from higher education to work*. LTSN Generic Centre.

HRDF. (2020). *Cultivate the internal talent: SMEs chapter*. HRDF Industry Intelligence Report No. 10/2020. Retrieved February 17, 2023, from https://hrdcorp.gov.my/wpcontent/uploads/2021/03/10_2020_Industry-Training-Intelligencereport.Pdf

HRDF Human Capital Report. (2019). *Skill shortages: Malaysians are lacking communication skills*. https://hrdcorp.gov.my/wp-content/uploads/2021/03/12.-issue_Sept02_2019-Human-Capital-Report-Skills-Shortages.pdf

Kamil, B. A. M., Rani, S. H. A., & Hasnan, N. (2023). *Talent management and digital transformation in the Malaysian SMEs' manufacturing sector*. In N. M. Suki, A. R. Mazlan, R. Azmi, N. A. Abdul Rahman, Z. Adnan, N. Hanafi, & R. Truell (Eds.), Strengthening Governance, Enhancing Integrity and Navigating Communication for Future Resilient Growth, vol 132. In *European Proceedings of Social and Behavioural Sciences* (pp. 148–161). European Publisher. https://doi.org/10.15405/epsbs.2023.11.02.12

Kassid, S. (2022). *What about us? Youth (UN) employment in times of COVID-19*. World Future Council. https://www.worldfuturecouncil.org/covid19-what-about-us/

Laar, E. V., Deursen, A. J. A. M. V., & Dijk, J. A. G. M. V. (2020). Determinants of 21st-century skills and 21st-century digital skills for workers: A systematic literature. *SAGE Open*, *10*, 2158244019900176.

Laar, E. V., Deursen, A. J. A. M. V., Dijk, J. A. G. M. V., & Haan, J. D. (2017). The relation between 21st-century skills and digital skills: A systematic literature review. *Computers in Human Behavior*, *72*, 577–588.

Lees, D. (2002). *Graduate employability: Literature review*. LTSN Generic Centre.

Little, B. (2001). Reading between the lines of graduate employment. *Quality in Higher Education*, *7*, 121–129.

Lugovsky, V. (2021). Industry 4.0: The beneficial trends and challenges for SMEs. *Forbes*. https://www.forbes.com/sites/forbesbusinesscouncil/2021/09/03/industry-40-the-beneficial-trends-and-challenges-for-smes/?sh=617d1d8293cb=

Malaysia Digital Economy Corporation. (2021). *Digital skills key to bolster workforce*. Retrieved February 17, 2023, from https://mdec.my/blog/?p=1074

McGunagle, D., & Zizka, L. (2020). Employability skills for 21st century STEM students: The employers' perspective. *Higher Education, Skills and Work-based Learning*, *10*, 1–22.

McKinsey. (2022). *What are Industry 4.0, the Fourth Industrial Revolution, and 4IR?* https://www.mckinsey.com/featured-insights/mckinsey-explainers/what-are-industry-4-0-the-fourth-industrial-revolution-and-4ir#/

moda.my.gov. (2019). *Devising IR 4.0-oriented education – MIDA | Malaysian Investment Development Authority*.

MPC. (2024). https://www.mpc.gov.my/mpc-news/initiative-to-develop-skilled-workforce

Musa, H., & Chinniah, M. (2016). *Malaysian SMEs development: Future and challenges on going green*. In 6th international research symposium in service management, IRSSM-6 2015, 11–15 August, 2015, UiTM Sarawak, Kuching, Malaysia.

Rahmat, M., Adnan, M., Haimi, A., & Mohtar, M. N. (2019). Industry 4.0 skillsets and 'career readiness': Can Malaysian University students face the future of work? In MNNF Network (Ed.), *Proceedings of the international invention, innovative & creative (InIIC) conference series 2/2019* (pp. 28–37). MNNF Network. https://ssrn.com/abstract=3511166

Robinson, J. P. (2022). What are employability skills? *The Workplace. A Fact Sheet. The Alabama Cooperative Extension System*, *1*, 1–3. https://www.middletowncityschools.com/media/studentservices/Information_Grade10_WhatAreEmployabilitySkills.pdf

Sajitha, B., Dahlman, C. J., Kanehira, N., & Tilmes, K. (2021). *The converging technology revolution and human capital: Potential and implications for South Asia*. World Bank.

Sidek, M., Razak, A., Samsol, A. F., & Hamdi, I. Industrial Revolution 4.0 integration in engineering education – Readiness case study of Diploma in Mechanical Engineering Program. *Jurnal Teknikal & Kajian Sosial (Juteks)*, *19*(1), 25–31.

Sofea, A. (2022). *What TVET needs is good dose of talent show*. Institute of Strategic and International Studies (ISIS), Malaysia. https://www.isis.org.my/2022/05/26/what-tvet-needs-isgood-dose-of-talent-show/

Stiwne, E. E., & Alves, M. G. (2010). Higher education and employability of graduates: Will Bologna make a difference? *European Educational Research Journal*,*9*, 32–44.

Talin, B. (2021). *23 skills of the future—Important skills for the jobs of 21st century*. https://morethandigital. info/en/23-skills-of-the-future-important-skills-for-the-jobs-of-21th-century/

UNESCO. (2017). *Towards quality assurance of technical and vocational education and training*. ISBN: 978-92-9223581-9. https://unesdoc.unesco.org/ark:/48223/pf0000259282

Vasileiadou, S. M. (2023). *Skills and competencies in the digital transformation era: The case of Greece* [M.Sc. thesis]. School of Science & Technology, Thessaloniki – Greece.

Yunus, M. Z. M., Mohamad, M., Bahari, A., & Ngadimin, N. F. (2024). Way forward future skills framework, strategies and action plan for Malaysian talent development. *International Journal of Future Education and Advances (IJFEA)*, *1*(1), 110–122.

6

DIGITAL FUTURE OF SMEs: TOWARDS SUCCESSFUL DIGITAL TRANSFORMATION

ABSTRACT

The chapter begins with a discussion of the transformative innovations that play a key role in the digital transformation of small and medium-sized enterprises (SMEs). Technological advancements like cloud computing, business process automation (BPA), artificial intelligence (AI), and others will play an ever-increasing role, but their development and use must be balanced with ethical considerations. In the future, organizations will be reliant on technologies such as AI for prediction, decision-making, new strategy development, and more. Therefore, ethical and legal concerns are crucial. This chapter will thus probe into those ethical concerns surrounding AI-based algorithms, and models. These ethical issues would require adaptability as the landscape evolves with technology. The chapter emphasizes the need for SMEs to be prepared and to adapt to new digital environments on a constant basis so as to ensure the successful implementation of digital transformation. This will prove that digital transformation is a reality, and not a fantasy for SMEs. They need to focus on having a well-defined digital strategy that is future-focussed if they wish to remain competitive and relevant in the digital era. This chapter also looks at one Malaysian-based company which had grown from being a small firm to becoming a multinational company. The case study illustrates how the company's use of technologies had helped it to expand its business and to improve efficiency. By adopting new technologies and by being adaptable, it is possible for Malaysian SMEs to prosper and succeed in the digital world.

Keywords: Transformative innovation; artificial intelligence; machine learning; generative AI; cyber ethics

1. INTRODUCTION

Transformative innovation refers to those existing systems, products, or services which had been transformed to become new ones so that they become more suitable, efficient, and effective to fulfil current needs and future requirements. Transformative innovation brings forth new concepts, it creates new markets, and it also revolutionizes the entire industry, thereby changing people's lifestyles. A few years back, people used to go to taxi stands to get a taxi, or they may order or book a taxi for their destination by calling a taxi company. With ride-hailing apps today, people can easily book their rides at any time, and from anywhere to anywhere they wish. This is one prominent illustration of transformative innovation which shows that ride-hailing services can disrupt the traditional taxi industry.

Other examples of transformative innovation include smartphones, which have revolutionized communication, entertainment, and productivity; electric vehicles, which are transforming transportation and energy consumption; cloud computing that has changed the way businesses store, process, and access data. Meanwhile, AI has made human tasks easier as it has the ability to automate certain manual tasks, enhance decision-making, and also personalize experiences. Another component, blockchain, has revolutionized financing approaches, transformed supply chain procedures, and also created digital identities for people. All these innovations go beyond incremental improvements; they offer the world profound changes which can impact both the individual's lifestyles and the world's economic structures.

In business, transformative innovations offer the industry numerous benefits. They can increase business efficiency by streamlining processes, reducing costs, and enhancing productivity (Smartbridge, 2020). With innovative products or services, companies can tap into unexplored markets, and generate new revenue streams (Anthony et al., 2019). First movers of digital transformation have a competitive advantage over the late adopters, thereby differentiating themselves from the competitors. Additionally, digital transformation offers businesses the ability to promote innovations that can improve customer experiences, personalization, and faster services. These improvements can, in turn, foster customer loyalty. Another significant benefit is market expansion.

As businesses find the platform to reach new audiences, they become more adept at exploring the broad global opportunities to expand, thereby breaking traditional boundaries. The next section will discuss some of the successful transformative innovations.

2. SUCCESSFUL TRANSFORMATIVE INNOVATION

2.1. Google

Google has revolutionized the way people access information today; it has made it possible for people to access answers to their questions with a single click. Today, the word, 'Googling' is a common word used as a form of looking to find facts online (Dieffenbacher, 2023). Advertisers find Google's ad services particularly appealing because of its innovative lead generation and advertising technology. This has been further strengthened by Google Caffeine which permits direct lead collections in AdWords ads. Through the acquisition of Urchin and the free analytics market, Google has impacted developers and SEO experts by solidifying its end-to-end control over sponsored search and analytics (Wordstream, 2021).

2.2. Facebook

Through diverse social media platforms, Facebook has revolutionized global communications by fundamentally changing the way people interact and connect (Dieffenbacher, 2023). With more than one billion active users, it has remained the world's most popular social media platform. It is able to influence people's daily routines, leaving behind a lasting impact on the digital landscape. Facebook's rebranding to Meta exemplifies its adoption of Clayton Christensen's disruption innovation theory, which only reflects its strategic shift to stay ahead in the evolving technological landscape. This move signifies a radical change in the company's operations and values, like its earlier pivot towards messaging apps. By acquiring Instagram in 2012, and WhatsApp in 2014, Facebook has strategically positioned itself towards adapting to the mobile-centric consumer shift. These acquisitions allow Facebook to disrupt itself before competitors could, demonstrating its commitment to transformative change, and its readiness to compete in new markets (Mulligan, 2021). Facebook's transition to Meta indicates another bold step it is taking in redefining its business focus. Its move towards the metaverse marks the next phase of its strategic evolution.

2.3. Netflix

Netflix began by revolutionizing the DVD rental industry with a convenient mail-out service. With the ability to recognize consumers' shifting preferences, Netflix had boldly transitioned to online streaming, thereby transforming entertainment consumption. By offering a vast library of movies and TV shows for instant streaming, Netflix had disrupted the services offered by traditional video rental stores, converting itself into a global streaming powerhouse. By investing heavily in technology and original contents, Netflix outperformed traditional movie studios and became a leading content creator.

3. TRANSFORMATIVE INNOVATION AND SMEs

The impact of transformative innovation can be especially significant for SMEs. Although SMEs often face challenges, such as limited resources, risk aversion, and legacy systems, the strategic adoption of new technologies can propel them to substantial growth. By leveraging on innovations like cloud computing and AI, the SME industries can automate tasks and manage their resources more effectively. This can elevate business operations and promote efficiency. E-commerce platforms and online payment systems have also opened up new revenue streams for SMEs to reach a broader set of audiences. The agility of smaller companies can also accelerate the implementation of new technologies, thereby providing them with a competitive edge over larger firms. The personalized services offered by technology allow customers to enhance their experiences and increase their personal satisfaction with the services, thereby improving customer loyalty. This would give SMEs the pathway to break into new markets, and the opportunity to expand. The other challenges faced by SMEs can be sorted out through collaborations, adaptability, and by leveraging on government support.

The theory of Industry 4.0 which includes the integration of cyber-physical systems, the internet of things (IoT), and advanced data analytics, is well aligned with the revolutionary breakthroughs outlined above. Industrial SMEs can benefit significantly from Industry 4.0 technologies (Raizada, 2024). These technologies enable real-time data gathering and analysis, predictive maintenance, and intelligent decision-making all of which can enhance operational efficiency with minimum downtime. Industrial SMEs that embrace Industry 4.0 can improve their production processes, optimize supply chain management, and increase overall competitiveness (Ernst & Frische, 2015). By eliminating their obsolete practices, SMEs thus bring about significant changes across the industries which also cause businesses to function more effectively. The list of technologies, their functions, the changes they have innovated, and how they are assisting SMEs in operating more effectively are further discussed.

3.1. Cloud Computing

Cloud technology enables SMEs to access scalable computing resources without heavy upfront investments. It enhances collaborations, data storage, and deployment applications. Cloud providers start by hosting virtual computers in enormous data centres which include tech giants like Amazon, Microsoft, and Google. In relation to this, SMEs do not have to worry about the risk associated with any of the physical infrastructure because these computers could be utilized on a pay-as-you-go basis, and they can be accessed over the internet (Jani, 2023; Owino, 2023). For example, a cloud-based accounting software called QuickBooks Online can be utilized by small firms to manage finances, payrolls, and client billings. The cloud solution allows firms to access financial data from anywhere, engage with clients in real time, and also provide automatic backups for data protection. These facilities help SMEs to expand their businesses, and to bring in more innovations without huge investments.

3.2. Business Process Automation

Automation is a process that streamlines repetitive tasks. It improves efficiency and reduces human errors, thus, SMEs can use automation to ease their workflows, customer interactions, and inventory management. BPA in SMEs would provide significant efficiency gains; it reduces the need for human labour across a variety of processes. SMEs can use conversational digital assistants for customer service. This process reduces agent workloads and improves reaction times.

In finance, BPA automates invoice processing, reduces errors, and speeds up payment cycles. In HR departments, it automates employee onboarding, contract generation, and training schedules. In supply chains and inventory management, automation solutions help to manage stock levels, process orders, and track shipments. In marketing aspect, efforts are boosted by automated email campaigns that carry personalized contents. The automation of data collection and analysis streamlines compliance and reporting, thereby lowering administrative overhead costs while assuring regulatory conformance. Despite these advantages, some concerns on automation of business process have emerged. They include the selection of suitable processes for automation and reducing its impact on human resources. To resolve these issues, careful planning, and the proper monitoring of key performance indicators (KPIs), are needed (Moreira et al., 2023).

3.3. Artificial Intelligence and Machine Learning

AI and machine learning (ML) can enhance decision-making, customer service, and predictive analytics. Some examples of AI applications are chatbots, recommendation engines, and personalized marketing. SMEs can use both the AI and ML elements to improve their operations and consumer interactions. AI-powered customer analytics can assist organizations in understanding client behaviour and preferences, thereby allowing them to offer tailored products and services to the customers (McKinsey, 2023; Raman & Mookherjee, 2023). Automating repetitive processes, such as inventory management, saves time and minimizes errors. It can lead to a 30% reduction in operational expenses for a small manufacturing company.

AI and ML also provide data-driven decision-making as demonstrated in a restaurant chain. This process can help restaurants to optimize their menu, ultimately leading to a 15% improvement in customer satisfaction. Real-world case studies have shown that with the assistance of AI chatbots, e-commerce has increased customer service, resulting in an increase of 40% inquiries. It was noted that an agricultural SME which had used AI-powered drones to increase crops was able to reap a higher yield of 20%. Taken together, the AI and ML technologies have enhanced efficiency, customer satisfaction, and profitability for SMEs (Mishrif & Khan, 2023).

3.4. Cybersecurity Technologies

With technological advancement, cybersecurity also has arisen issue. As cyber threats increase, SMEs would require more robust security solutions. Therefore, it is essential that they implement firewalls, encryptions, and other forms of threat detection tools. SMEs have increasingly focussed on enhancing cybersecurity measures to protect their data and operations.

In Wales, for instance, SMEs have adopted various cybersecurity practices, including regular security checks on Internet-connected devices, and in securing social media accounts. They implemented intelligent software packages to safeguard data. Such practices require significant investments and a large pool of skilled personnel. To address these challenges, the Welsh Government (WG) offered funding and training programmes to improve SMEs' cybersecurity threats. An additional measure taken by the WG was collaboration with cybersecurity experts. Service providers were encouraged to keep SMEs updated on the latest threats and technologies. Meanwhile, SMEs are also leveraging on other resources, such as the National Cyber Security Centre guidelines, the Cyber Essentials scheme, and the Cyber Security Information Sharing Partnership as safety measures to enhance their cybersecurity defence (Rawindaran et al., 2023). SMEs can use similar cyber security measures to protect themselves from hackers and cyber-attacks.

In Malaysia, the Cyber Security Act 2024 (ACT 854) came into enforcement on 26 August 2024 with the aim to build up Malaysia's cyber defences and to improve resilience against cyber threats. Under this act, the 11 National Critical Information Infrastructure (NCII) sectors including government; healthcare; energy; agriculture; information, communication, and digital science; technology and innovation; banking and finance; defence and national security; transportation; water and waste management; and sewage treatment need to conduct comprehensive cybersecurity risk assessment annually. Also, any organization including SMEs or individuals offering cybersecurity services must obtain licence to ensure they are qualified to provide cybersecurity-related services. Therefore, this law aims to protect the NCII entities and the country from increasing and sophisticated cyber threats and attacks (Medina, 2024).

3.5. Online Payments and E-commerce Platforms

SMEs can extend their scope by adopting e-commerce platforms. They offer secure online payment options which facilitate global sales and customer conveniences. To date, SMEs are leveraging on various e-commerce platforms to enhance their online presence as a measure to cater to the growing demands of online shopping. Key platforms such as WordPress WooCommerce, Shopify, BigCommerce, Magento, OpenCart, Wix, PrestaShop, SiteGiant, Drupal Commerce, and e-commerce offer unique features that cater to different business needs. These platforms offer user-friendly interfaces, diverse customization options, robust payment processing, and various scalable solutions. All these facilities enable SMEs to streamline operations, and to deliver seamless shopping experiences to customers. With the right e-commerce platform, Malaysian SMEs would be able to thrive further in the digital era. This would, in turn, promote and sustain growth and competitiveness within an increasingly online marketplace (SuperKeat, 2023).

3.6. Virtual Workspaces and Remote Collaboration Tools

With the rise of remote work, it is evident that virtual workspaces, video conferencing, and project management tools have also become important. They enable teams to collaborate effortlessly, regardless of their geographic locations (Rawindaran et al., 2023). Tools such as Microsoft Teams, Slack, and Zoom enable real-time communications and collaborations, thereby breaking down traditional barriers. Remote work provides employees with a better work–life balance and work flexibility. These can improve work efficiency as well as elevate job satisfaction, ultimately leading to higher productivity of workers.

Remote work also lowers operation costs by reducing the need for physical office space and commute. In this way, businesses can reinvest such savings in other areas of operations and productions. The various tools are critical components of digital transformation as they streamline procedures and increase productivity (Dixit, 2023). Another benefit of remote work is cloud-based document sharing, and project management solutions, both of which enable real-time collaborations which also enhance coordination and productivity. With the reduction in commute and transportation, energy consumption is lowered, and sustainability is enhanced. In this regard, SMEs can use remote work as a concept for innovative businesses to use digital workspaces as a means to preserve a united and diverse organizational culture.

4. NEXT-GEN SOLUTIONS FOR SMEs

As discussed in the examples of successful transformative innovations earlier, Google has been recognized for its ability to organize and make information accessible to everyone. It may even be used to confront the 'innovator's dilemma' in which even well-managed companies falter in the face of technological competition. While Google succeeds at maintaining breakthroughs, disruptive inventions such as OpenAI's ChatGPT provide customers with brand new forms of consumption. Despite its shortcomings, ChatGPT can still disrupt the market by changing the way consumers seek information (Azhar, 2023).

These are powerful innovations that create new markets and value networks, which would eventually displace all the established market-leading firms, products, and alliances. These innovations often start in niche markets, and they would then flourish further to dominate mainstream markets. Some of these technologies are discussed in the following sections.

4.1. Generative AI

AI which creates materials using generative models is known as generative AI. It uses sophisticated algorithms and neural networks to create new contents which comprise of vast amounts of data that include text, photos, audio, and videos (Becher, 2024). SMEs can use generative AI to create high quality contents on social media, blogs, and websites. They can also use these contents to maintain a strong online presence with less amount of effort. AI can also be used for graphic designing, such as creating logo and posts while videos can also be added to enhance the usefulness of generative AI. It is clear that AI can be used as a customer care support for 24 hours to answer general enquiries. This gives the human resources department more time to perform other complex tasks. AI bots that generate contents can also produce trade stocks, music, and artwork while performing administrative duties. This technical breakthrough has a significant impact on how today's leaders and employees perform their daily activities. It also enhances the toolset of modern corporate operations (Shields, 2024).

4.2. Blockchain

Blockchain is a decentralized digital ledger technology. It can record transactions across several computers in such a way that they cannot be changed later. This process offers transparency, security, and immutability (Frizzo-Barker et al., 2020). Industries like healthcare and supply chain management adopt this technology to store patient records due to its secure storage and sharing feature, thereby ensuring privacy and HIPAA compliance. Drug traceability, for instance, ensures the authenticity and safety of pharmaceuticals through the supply chain. In short, blockchain improves transparency and traceability by keeping a permanent record of the whole supply chain. It also prevents counterfeiting by validating product authenticity at every level.

In the case of SMEs, blockchain offers them a very affordable and convenient way to conduct their transactions such as to make and receive payments efficiently and securely. From the secure and dependable platforms provided, blockchain enables SMEs from underdeveloped economies to gain access to global markets so as to make cross-border transactions (Bizama, 2022). By using a decentralized ledger, blockchain ensures that all transactions are transparent and immutable, thereby enhancing trust among stakeholders. This technology eliminates the need for intermediaries, such as banks, and it significantly reduces transaction costs while increasing operational efficiency.

Further, blockchain can streamline supply chain operations by providing real-time tracking which also confirms the verification of goods, reduces frauds, and also improves inventory management (Twendee Blog, 2024).

4.3. Internet of Things

The IoT has emerged as a transformative technology. It connects various objects, such as physical devices, buildings, and vehicles, to existing information networks. By integrating these objects into a cohesive network, the IoT serves as a catalyst for the creation of new markets and value networks. This revolutionizes economies and societies. The high expectations placed on the IoT solutions stemmed from their potential to foster disruptive innovations for sustainability across various sectors (Nasiri et al., 2017).

The use of the IoT increases the overall competitiveness of SMEs through the monitoring of equipment, and the automating of routine tasks. By delivering real-time data and insights, the IoT thus lowers the operating costs of SMEs, such as energy consumption and maintenance expenses (Thinc, 2024). In supply chain management, the IoT simplifies operations by allowing real-time tracking, and the monitoring of items. This decreases delays and enhances inventory control. The IoT also helps SMEs to create new business models For example, subscription-based services or pay-per-use models create new revenue streams for SMEs. It also helps SMEs to implement sustainable practices by monitoring resource utilization and by minimizing wastes and thereby contribute to environmental goals (World Economic Forum, 2022a, 2022b). All these benefits enable SMEs to remain competitive within an ever changing business environment. Clearly, the IoT has potential to re-revolutionize business markets, and to drive the emergence of sustainability-driven disruptive innovations (Nasiri, 2016).

4.4. The 5G Technology

Advancements like the 5G technology offer faster speeds, lower latency, and greater connectivity. It enables real-time data transmission and communication. It facilitates telemedicine in healthcare, supports autonomous vehicles in the automotive sector, and enhances traffic management in smart cities. It also supports the integration of IoT devices, which leads to improved urban planning, better energy management, enhanced public safety, and higher quality of life. The 5G technology impact is better felt by sectors like manufacturing, entertainment, and logistics because it can fundamentally alter how businesses work (Becher, 2024).

Due to the faster speed that the 5G technology offers, SMEs can thus advance to technologies like AI, and the IoT to make better data-driven decisions. This process can save cost and energy. The 5G technology also creates new revenue sources through innovations, such as remote work, virtual reality experiences, and smart products. SMEs can also improve customer experience by providing faster response time, personalized services, and better digital interactions (Davis, 2019). The early adoption of 5G can facilitate SMEs' competitiveness by enabling them to respond faster and swifter to market changes within the digital economy.

5. DIGITAL TRANSFORMATION AND ETHICS

The advent of digital technology has raised the concern of ethics, in lieu of responsible and equitable growth and the digital transformation of Malaysia likewise, presents a wide range of ethical issues that are in need of attention and resolution.

5.1. Cyber Ethics

The first ethical issue concerns data privacy and security. Privacy protection and the appropriate utilization of personal information are the foundations of ethical conduct in the digital world. Everyone has a responsibility to respect each other's personal information, and to refrain from breaching or purposefully causing harm to another person. Data threats occur when individuals or groups turn to hacking, stealing, or infecting the digital assets (IP) of another person with malicious software and viruses (Wahab, 2021). As the nation's digital footprints expand significantly, it is also becoming increasingly exposed to data breaches and identity theft.

The digital footprints can produce a huge amount of data which are obtained from browsing history to location data, and online purchase data to social media activity. If there are data breaches, hackers can gain access to all the sensitive information of users, such as names, addresses, banking details, and others alike which can lead to identity theft. Using the stolen information, hackers can open new accounts, make purchases using users' bank accounts, and they may even commit crimes. The outcome can cause social embarrassment, and the issue may take a long time to be resolved. In this regard, cyber ethics are crucial and they should be strictly adhered to when different parties are involved in such situations. The term, 'Cyber Ethics' refers to the code of conduct that ought to be practised on the internet. It serves as guidance for the individual users to feel safe while engaging in positive, sensible, and ethical online behaviours that are based on common sense and good judgement. Cyber ethics and its practices can contribute to a favourable cyber environment, and so, a strong digital economy for Malaysia.

5.2. Transparency and Cybersecurity

While handling users' data, there must be transparency to indicate to the users as to how and why their data are being used, with their consent. This will cultivate a strong relationship between SME owners and their customers. It is an ethical obligation for SMEs to prevent unauthorized access to or use of customers' data. Raising awareness about the significance of cybersecurity is thus essential since cybersecurity and business ethics are inter-related. In business, strong cybersecurity procedures are crucial for protecting sensitive data (Klein, 2022). While business ethics ensure that ethical considerations are adhered to, they also upkeep the integrity of businesses when using the information derived from modern technologies. This means that greater organizational accountability is necessary in data management to ensure that there is compliance with the legal and ethical ramifications of data ownership. Additionally, ethical decision-making also contributes to the enduring sustainability of an organization because it facilitates the application of digitalization solutions that align with employees' values and principles.

6. ETHICS IN AI DEVELOPMENT AND USAGE

The AI market is projected to reach US$184 billion in the year 2024 (Statista, 2024), and countries all over the world are aggressively developing and implementing AI technologies. Most organizations are heavily investing in AI, or they are planning to invest in AI technologies as part of their digital transformation initiatives. AI, ML, and automation provide vast benefits to organization in terms of operational efficiency, cost reduction, reduced errors, improved decision-making, and more. Nevertheless, there are still issues surrounding the development and use of AI technologies. One of the key issues is the ethical issues associated with the technologies.

AI systems should be trained with unbiased data. This means that if the data used were skewed or underrepresented, then the technology is likely to generate biased decisions as an outcome. This would affect ethical decision-making.

Moreover, the dataset that was used for training the AI systems must also be diverse and representative of the country. If the majority of the data used had been derived from one particular ethnicity or gender, the prediction or outcome generated would also be biased and unbalanced. For example, a research conducted at Carnegie Mellon University noted that the online advertising system of Google was inclined towards displaying positions that offer higher salaries to males than to females (IBM, 2021). Such an outcome may have been affected by gender-biased data.

Obviously, AI developers should pay attention to the design of AI algorithms in order to prevent discriminatory, unfair, and biased results which could harm certain groups of users. Therefore, when using AI systems, the companies involved must maintain transparency in terms of how the algorithms work, and how decisions are made. This would increase the confidence of the people providing their data. Ultimately, they would be more confident in following the decisions generated by the system. When a company is using an AI system, it should take the responsibility for any decisions made by the system. The company should conduct proper research before implementing the system and should be accountable for the actions of the AI systems.

7. ETHICAL GUIDELINES FOR SMEs CONSIDERING AI SYSTEMS

Any breach in data use could lead to serious consequences for SMEs and their customers. Thus, data should be collected and used ethically. Informed consent should be obtained from the customers or other parties for using their data in the AI systems. The data should be collected and stored following the data protection policies. In Malaysia, all companies including SMEs should comply with the Personal Data Protection (Amendment) Bill 2024 as it provides guidelines on how to process personal and sensitive data. Furthermore, the data privacy policies of SMEs should be regularly updated as per the latest government regulations. SMEs should also provide proper training to their employees regarding the ethical use of AI systems to support ethical decision-making.

SMEs should be proactive in conducting extensive research when developing or purchasing AI systems. They should have proper consultations and discussions with the system provider so as to ensure that the system is free from bias and discrimination. SMEs should also regularly monitor and audit the algorithms and decisions made by the system so as to check for any biased pattern of results that could demonstrate unfairness or discrimination. Similarly, SMEs should follow the industry guidelines or the ethical frameworks provided when implementing AI systems in their businesses.

7.1. Cyber Ethics and Initiatives in Malaysia

To tackle the ethical concerns, multiple initiatives have been developed in Malaysia, including the National Cyber Ethics Initiative which aims to cultivate virtuous principles, ethical behaviours, self-control, and a sense of accountability among the consumers of digital technology in Malaysia. Additionally, Cybersecurity Malaysia has also been proactive in providing parents and children with educational materials on cyber principles. By integrating ethical considerations into their cybersecurity strategies, SMEs can promote confidence, reduce shortcomings, and assure their customers and staff of a secure digital world (Wahab, 2021).

On 20 September 2024, Malaysian government launched Artificial Intelligence Governance and Ethical Guidelines framework. The framework aims to inform the users of AI systems, AI-based software or technology developers and providers, the policymakers and the public about the do's and don'ts of developing and using AI technology. The framework is based on seven principles namely fairness, reliability, inclusiveness, transparency, safety and control, privacy and security, and accountability (Koya, 2024). The framework would serve as guidelines for all the parties including SMEs to ensure the safe and ethical use of AI in their businesses. The government also intends to establish a dedicated office, National Artificial Intelligence Office (NAIO) and data commission to protect data and promote the use of data centres in Malaysia.

8. MAKING DIGITAL TRANSFORMATION A REALITY FOR SMEs

Digital transformation can definitely become a reality for SMEs. To achieve this, SMEs need a strong digital strategy to act as guidance and direction. This starts from the stage of identifying suitable digital tools to the continuous monitoring of the tools for further improvements. Digital transformation is a continuous journey while digital strategy is the key to support this journey successfully. Since SMEs are constrained by their limited resources, they may think that investing in digitalization is not necessary at this point of time. However, the truth is that it is important to invest in the latest technologies such as robotic process automation, cloud computing, and AI because of the benefits that SMEs can reap. They are necessary to enable SMEs to achieve their internal and external business objectives. For instance, with the implementation of the latest technologies, SMEs can experience the internal improvement of process efficiency, employee effectiveness, and cost reduction. Alternatively, SMEs can also experience external improvements manifested through online sales increase, higher customer reach, and better brand visibility. However, SMEs must make optimal use of their available resources in order to achieve such objectives.

As part of their digital strategy, SMEs should conduct proper investigations on the digital resources or tools which are currently being used, to what extent are these being used, and what are their impacts on business performances. This would highlight the performance of the current level of digitalization in the company. The outcome derived from the investigation would also help SMEs to identify the tools which should be implemented in order to improve business functions and performance.

Based on the needs identified, SMEs can set the objectives that they want to achieve by implementing the new digital technologies. For instance, the objective set can be, to have 30% improvement in employee productivity (investment in automation tools can help to achieve this), or 50% improvement in online sales (use of digital marketing tools can help to achieve this). Most importantly, SMEs need to set up KPIs to monitor the achievement of those objectives. For example, improvement in customer service can be tracked through the number of customer complaints solved within a particular period of time. Similarly, the online sales and customer satisfaction can be monitored through the increase in website traffic, or the increase in customer ratings via Google analytics. This output should be reviewed frequently to verify whether the objectives have been met or whether further adjustments are required.

Furthermore, when new technologies are implemented, the employees should also have the competence to use these technologies. If they do not have sufficient digital skills, they may not be able to use the tools to their full potential. Therefore, SMEs need to upskill and reskill their employees. On the other hand, hiring new employees who have expertise in the field would be an alternative option (Nyakarundi, 2024). In this regard, it is important that SMEs have a strong digital strategy to make digital transformation a reality since it enables SMEs to invest, utilize, monitor, and seek continuous improvements.

9. CASE EXAMPLE: FROM ONE SMALL HARDWARE STORE TO A BILLION DOLLAR HOME IMPROVEMENT ENTERPRISE

9.1. Company Background

Mr.DIY was started by two brothers. It began as a small hardware store in Kuala Lumpur, Malaysia in the year 2005. Within a few years, Mr.DIY had expanded to other locations. In the year 2008, a Mr.DIY store was opened inside Aeon

Mall. From then on, the company partnered with other stores such as Giant and Tesco. It began to make its brand name visible, and it attracted more customers. The company was public-listed on the Kuala Lumpur Stock Exchange (Bursa Malaysia) in 2020. Today, it has over 1,000 stores in Malaysia, and the average size of the stores is 10,000 square feet. The store carries about 18,000 varieties of products. The company has also expanded into international markets, such as Indonesia, the Philippines, Thailand, Brunei, India, Indonesia, Spain, Singapore, Vietnam, and Cambodia. These stores are expanding rapidly with over 3,900 branches worldwide. In 2022, the company also opened Mr.DIY Plus, a 30,000 square feet store at MidValley Mall, one of the busiest shopping malls in Malaysia. The company's aim is to provide essential home improvement products at the lowest prices. Their branches at various locations provide a greater convenience to people to purchase their needed products at their convenient locations. With the huge variety of products ranging from furniture, electricals, stationeries, hardware to homeware, customers can find anything in the store (Macro Ops, 2022).

9.2. Power of Data Analytics at Mr.DIY

The company has a great digital strategy and has invested in several technologies. Mr.DIY uses data analytics intensively for its business expansion. For instance, before opening a new store, the company gathers data about the location, population, and residential numbers. These data were then analysed to determine the perfect site for the new branches. Furthermore, the results of the analytics also helped the company to determine the size of the store to be opened. As mentioned earlier, the average size of a full Mr.DIY store is about 10,000 square feet, but in certain smaller locations and communities, a full store may not be necessary, so the company opens a Mr.DIY express which is about 4,000 square feet. These decisions were made and supported heavily with the help of data analytics. The data analytics also helped the company to implement data-driven business strategies, such as the opening of Mr Dollar, a global fixed price retailing business model where all the products in the store carry a low fixed price of either RM5 or RM2. The company's research on high and increasing toy prices also motivated them to open Mr Toys which sells quality toys at an affordable price (Moh, 2021).

9.3. E-commerce @ Mr.DIY

Understanding the growing importance of e-commerce, Mr.DIY started its online presence in the year 2018 on Shopee. Subsequently, the company implemented the 'click and collect model' where customers placed their orders online, and then collect the products at the nearest Mr.DIY store. Since the company has several branches in various locations, this was easily achieved. Through this strategy, the company was able to save on logistics and shipping costs. In the year 2019, the company invested in designing and building an e-commerce robotic warehouse which was launched in 2021. With the robotic warehouse, the company was able to fulfil the online orders much faster, and better than the manual system. This incurred a 200% increase in operational efficiency, doing away with human errors. The automated robotic warehouse was designed to accommodate huge varieties of products as stocks which enabled online customers to have wide choices (Mr.DIY, 2021).

9.4. Lessons Learnt

Mr.DIY is an exceptional example that can motivate SMEs to learn about how a small company could expand and flourish to become a billion-dollar business. Through the adoption of AI and other digital technologies, Mr.DIY had implemented a clear digital strategy to transform business with the help of latest technologies. With this clear objective, the company had made huge investments in data analytics and the e-commerce arena. The use of digital tools, and data-driven strategies had also enabled the company to expand its business, reach more customers, and gain brand visibility and loyalty. The company is also embracing the fourth industrial revolution by investing in advanced technologies such as robotics as seen in the robotic warehouse which accelerated the online purchase process, and satisfied customers by delivering low priced and good quality products in a timely manner.

10. CHAPTER SUMMARY

This chapter started with a discussion of some of the transformative innovations that had changed the world including global businesses. Technologies such as AI, ML, cloud computing, BPA, etc., were explained. These tools can be used by SMEs to improve efficiency, reduce operation cost, and improve overall business performance. The chapter also emphasized that generative AI, blockchain, and the IoT should be adopted by SMEs because they provide powerful solutions to current business needs. The chapter further looked at the issue of ethics related to digital transformation. It was mentioned that the use of AI can lead to several ethical issues, hence some guidance was provided for SMEs to implement.

To date, the Malaysian government has also implemented initiatives such as the National Cyber Ethics, and is involved in the development of National Artificial Intelligence Governance and the Code of Ethics Guidelines to support the various parties involved in the development and use of AI technologies. This chapter had stressed that implementing a digital strategy is important for SMEs if they aim to succeed in the digital transformation process. With all the issues and resolutions highlighted, it can be restated here that digital transformation is not a fantasy for SMEs anymore. Indeed it is real and feasible for SMEs and various actions that SMEs can take have been informed. To fortify the possibilities for SMEs, the case of Mr.DIY was then used as an example to show that with the right goals, and a proper digital strategy, digital transformation can convert a small business to become a conglomerate with tremendous growth and global presence.

REFERENCES

Anthony, S., Trotter, A., & Schwartz, E. (2019). *The top 20 business transformations of the last decade*. https://hbr.org/2019/09/the-top-20-business-transformations-of-the-last-decade

Azhar, A. (2023). *Google and the disruptive innovator*. https://www.exponentialview.co/p/google-and-the-disruptive-innovator

Becher, B. (2024, January 24). *Disruptive technology: 10 examples to know | Built In*. https://builtin.com/articles/disruptive-technology

Bizama, G. (2022, January 26). *Industry 4.0: The beneficial trends and challenges for SMEs*. https://www.forbes.com/sites/forbesbusinesscouncil/2021/09/03/industry-40-the-beneficial-trends-and-challenges-for-smes/

Davis, G. (2019, June 17). *How 5G mobile technology will help your small business – Small business UK*. https://smallbusiness.co.uk/how-5g-mobile-technology-will-help-your-small-business-2547877/

Dieffenbacher, S. (2023, July 10). *18 disruptive innovation examples 2023 – Digital leadership AG*. https://digitalleadership.com/blog/disruptive-innovation-examples/

Dixit, P. (2023, August 4). *The future of work: Remote collaboration and digital transformation – TIU Consulting*. https://www.tiuconsulting.com/digital-transformation/the-future-of-work-remote-collaboration-and-digital-transformation/

Ernst, F., & Frische, P. (2015). Industry 4.0/Industrial Internet of Things – Related technologies and requirements for a successful digital transformation: An investigation of manufacturing businesses worldwide. *SSRN Electronic Journal*. https://doi.org/10.2139/SSRN.2698137

Frizzo-Barker, J., Chow-White, P. A., Adams, P. R., Mentanko, J., Ha, D., & Green, S. (2020). Blockchain as a disruptive technology for business: A systematic review. *International Journal of Information Management*, *51*, 102029. https://doi.org/10.1016/J.IJINFOMGT.2019.10.014

IBM. (2021). AI bias examples. https://www.ibm.com/think/topics/shedding-light-on-ai-bias-with-real-world-examples

Jani, D. (2023, February 13). *What SME businesses benefit from cloud computing?*. https://www.softwareadvice.co.uk/blog/3452/business-benefits-cloud-computing

Klein, A. Z. (2022). Ethical issues of digital transformation. *Organizações & Sociedade*, *29*(102), 443–448. https://doi.org/10.1590/1984-92302022V29N0020EN

Koya, Z. (2024, September 21). *Keeping AI use in check*. https://www.thestar.com.my/news/nation/2024/09/21/keeping-ai-use-in-check

Macro Ops: Unparalleled Investing Research. (2022). *Mr. DIY: How two brothers turned one store into a $5B Empire*. https://macro-ops.com/blog/mr-diy-how-two-brothers-turned-one-store-into-a-5b-empire

McKinsey. (2023, January 8). *Generative AI in fashion*. https://www.mckinsey.com/industries/retail/our-insights/generative-ai-unlocking-the-future-of-fashion

Medina, A. F. (2024, August 30). *Malaysia's Cyber Security Act 2024: What businesses need to know*. https://www.aseanbriefing.com/news/malaysias-cyber-security-act-2024-what-businesses-need-to-know/#:~:text=The%20Cyber%20Security%20Act%202024,a%20license%20from%20the%20authorities

Mishrif, A., & Khan, A. (2023). Technology adoption as survival strategy for small and medium enterprises during COVID-19. *Journal of Innovation and Entrepreneurship*, 12(1), 1–23. https://doi.org/10.1186/S13731-023-00317-9/TABLES/4

Moh, J. (2021, August 19). *Data analytics – The tool behind Mr DIY's success*. https://thesun.my/business-news/data-analytics-the-tool-behind-mr-diy-s-success-FE8226474

Moreira, S., Mamede, H. S., & Santos, A. (2023). Business process automation in SMEs. *Lecture Notes in Business Information Processing, 464*, 426–437. https://doi.org/10.1007/978-3-031-30694-5_31.

Mr. DIY. (2021). MR. DIY launches e-commerce robotic warehouse in Malaysia!. https://www.mrdiy.com/mrdiy-launches-e-commerce-robotic-warehouse-in-malaysia

Mulligan, M. (2021, October 29). *Facebook is about to disrupt itself out of existence … again*. https://www.midiaresearch.com/blog/facebook-is-about-to-disrupt-itself-out-of-existenceagain

Nasiri, M. (2016). *Internet of things as an enabler in disruptive innovation for sustainability*. https://lutpub.lut.fi/handle/10024/129886

Nasiri, M., Tura, N., & Ojanen, V. (2017, January, 1–10). *Developing disruptive innovations for sustainability: A review on impact of internet of things (IOT) [Conference presentation]*. In *Portland International Conference on Management of Engineering and Technology* (PICMET), Portland, OR, USA, 09-13 July 2017, pp. 1–10, doi: 10.23919/PICMET.2017.8125369.

Nyakarundi, H. (2024, April 3). *Digital strategy for SMEs – ARED technology solutions*. https://aredgroup.com/what-smes-need-to-know-about-digital-strategy/ared

Owino, R. (2023, July 27). *7 key technology innovations transforming modern businesses*. https://pctechmag.com/2023/07/key-technology-innovations-transforming-modern-businesses/ruth

PwC. (2024). *What does 5G mean for enterprises*. https://www.pwc.com/us/en/industries/tmt/5g/enterprise.html

Raizada, A. (2024). *The rise of Industry 4.0: From automation to digital transformation*. https://copperdigital.com/blog/industry-4-0-evolution-automation-digital-transformation/

Raman, R., & Mookherjee, U. K. (2023). Revolutionizing Retail: Empowering Personalized Shopping with Advanced Algorithms. In *IEEE Technology & Engineering Management Conference – Asia Pacific* (TEMSCON-ASPAC), Bengaluru, India, 14-16 December 2023, pp. 1–5. doi: 10.1109/TEMSCON-ASPAC59527.2023.10531538.

Rawindaran, N., Jayal, A., Prakash, E., & Hewage, C. (2023). Perspective of small and medium enterprise (SME's) and their relationship with government in overcoming cybersecurity challenges and barriers in Wales. *International Journal of Information Management Data Insights*, *3*(2), 100191. https://doi.org/10.1016/J.JJIMEI.2023.100191.

Shields, K. D. (2024). Transformative or disruptive?: exploring the impact of generative AI on leadership. [Master's thesis, ZHAW School of Management and Law, Institute of Innovation and Entrepreneurship]. https://doi.org/10.21256/ZHAW-30469

Smartbridge. (2020). *Modernization, transformation and innovation in business*. https://smartbridge.com/modernization-transformation-innovation-business/

Statista (2024). Artificial Intelligence – World Wide. Statista Market Insights. https://www.statista.com/outlook/tmo/artificial-intelligence/worldwide

SuperKeat. (2023, November 6). *The ultimate list: The top 10 ecommerce platforms for SMEs in Malaysia – JustSimple Malaysia*. https://www.justsimple.com.my/top-ecommerce-platforms-for-smes-in-malaysia/

Thinc. (2024). *How can the internet of things benefit SMEs?* https://www.wearethinc.com/in-focus/how-can-the-internet-of-things-benefit-smes/

Twendee Blog. (2024). *Blockchain technology for small and medium enterprises (SMEs)*. https://blog.twendeesoft.com/blockchain/blockchain-technology-for-small-and-medium-enterprises-smes/

Wahab, A. (2021, September 28). *Advocating cyber ethics among Malaysian netizens – BizTech Times*. https://biztechtimes.com.my/2021/09/28/advocating-cyber-ethics-among-malaysian-netizens/

Wordstream. (2021, November 18). *Google: The king of disruptive technology*. https://www.wordstream.com/blog/ws/2010/01/29/google-disruptive-technology

World Economic Forum. (2022a). How blockchain accelerates small business growth and development. https://www.weforum.org/agenda/2022/01/how-blockchain-accelerates-small-business-growth-and-development/

World Economic Forum. (2022b). IoT can help small and medium businesses implement sustainability measures. https://www.weforum.org/agenda/2022/07/iot-small-medium-businesses-profitable-sustainable/

ABOUT THE AUTHORS

Farzana Parveen Tajudeen is a Senior Lecturer in the Department of Decision Science, Faculty of Business and Economics, Universiti Malaya, Malaysia. She is a member of the Association for Information Systems. Her research interests include artificial intelligence in business, internet of things adoption and impact, digital transformation, fintech, social media impact, and mHealth applications. She has published papers in various Web of Science journals such as International Journal of Human–Computer Interaction, European Journal of Innovation Management, Information & Management, Management Decisions, Telematics and Informatics, Industrial Management and Data Systems, Social Science Computer Review, International Journal of Mobile Communications, Sustainability, etc.

Sedigheh Moghavvemi is an Associate Professor of Technology Management and Entrepreneurship at the Faculty of Business & Economics at the Universiti Malaya. Her work has circulated internationally. Her research experience includes business and management, technological capability in Fourth Industrial Revolution, technology adoption, innovation management, smart tourism, and social media. She worked on different research and consultancies on entrepreneurship, marketing, and human resources, and the results were published in peer-reviewed journals.

Thinaranjeney Thirumoorthi is a Senior Lecturer in the Management and Marketing Department, Faculty of Business and Economics, Universiti Malaya. She started her career as a lecturer in 2016 and currently teaching Principles of Marketing, Strategic Marketing, Marketing Management, International Business Management, Tourism Management, Global Marketing, and Hospitality Management for both undergraduate and postgraduate programmes besides supervising PhD and Master's students. Her main research areas are backpacking tourism, medical tourism, gastronomic tourism, scuba diving tourism, homestay, community-based tourism, and city branding.

Seuk Wai Phoong is an Associate Professor in the Department of Decision Science, Faculty of Business and Economics, Universiti Malaya, Malaysia. She also acts as the Coordinator for the Student Holistic Empowerment programme. She obtained her highest academic qualification, PhD in Statistics from Universiti Sains Malaysia, Malaysia. She is a member of the Malaysian Mathematical Science Society (PERSAMA). Her research interests include applied statistics, econometrics, time series analysis, bibliometric analysis, and education. She has led 6 research projects out of 18 research grants. She has published papers in various Web of Science (WoS) and Scopus journals, such as *Sage Open*, *Artificial Intelligence Review*, *Humanities and Social Science*, *Mathematics*, *International Journal of Mobile Communications*, *Environmental Science and Pollution Research*, *Energies*, *Symmetry*, *Journal of Psychoactive Drugs*, *Journal of Retailing and Consumer Services*, etc. She is also an Academic Editor for several journals, including *PLOS One* (WoS, Q2), *Computer Vision Studies*, and *Asian Journal of Managerial Science*. She teaches Business Statistics and Quantitative Analysis for Business at the undergraduate level and Research Methodology, Statistical Analysis, and Operational Research at the postgraduate level.

Elya Nabila Binti Abdul Bahri is a Senior Lecturer at the Department of Economics, Faculty of Business and Economics, Universiti Malaya. She received her PhD in Economics from Universiti Kebangsaan Malaysia, Master of Economics and Bachelor of Economics from Universiti Malaya. Her research expertise includes macroeconomics, labour economics, development economics, financial economics, international economics, and applied econometrics. Her current research is on labour economics, retirees' wellbeing, food security, and financial economics.

Printed and bound by CPI Group (UK) Ltd, Croydon, CR0 4YY

17/09/2026

14964132-0001